Abraham Tucker

Freewill, foreknowledge and fate

A fragment

Abraham Tucker

Freewill, foreknowledge and fate
A fragment

ISBN/EAN: 9783337257507

Printed in Europe, USA, Canada, Australia, Japan

Cover: Foto ©Lupo / pixelio.de

More available books at **www.hansebooks.com**

FREEWILL,

FOREKNOWLEDGE,

AND

FATE.

A

FRAGMENT.

By EDWARD SEARCH, Esq;

Unde hæc est Fatis avolsa Voluntas.   LUCRET.

Hunc Naturam vocas, Fatum, Fortunam: omnia ejusdem Dei nomina sunt, varie utentis sua potestate.
                                    SENECA de Benef.

Others reason'd high of Knowledge, Fate, and Will:
Fixt Fate, Freewill, Foreknowledge absolute,
And found no end, in wandring mazes lost.
                                    MILTON.

LONDON:
Printed for R. and J. DODSLEY, in Pall-Mall.
MDCCLXIII.

TO

The READER.

ON revisiting *Alma Mater Oxoniensis* after a long absence, among many noble edifices entirely new to me, I observed an elegant range of chambers at *Magdalen*, on either end of which there projected two rows of rough stones from top to bottom ready to fasten in with future walls that might be run up against them; and chimnies were worked between for the accommodation of future chambers that might hereafter rise out of the adjacent ground. But as the said adjacent ground was smoothed into a neat parterre, and I saw no preparation for further erections, I could look upon the projector as having designed only to exhibit the fragment of a building.

Being at St. *Mary*'s one *Sunday*, I heard a learned and excellent discourse on three out of five sub-divisions of the second head of a treatise in defence of the Protestant Cause. I was told the first head had been delivered three years before, and it might probably come to the Preacher's turn to give the two remaining sub-divisions about three years hence: so considering how fluctuating a body the congregation consisted of, and supposing the Preacher knew their taste, I concluded it customary to present them with the fragment of a Dissertation.

Every body knows the prodigious demand for Magazines, which are little else than bundles of various and discordant fragments; and compositions of all kinds, not excepting Dictionaries, find greater vent when broken into numbers, than when delivered entire.

Having such precedents, as well of learned as simple, to keep me in countenance, I need no farther apology for exhibiting a Fragment to public view; especially since it can scarce be called so, when considered in itself: for I have pursued my subject as thoroughly as I was able, and brought it to a conclusion; so that

To the READER.

that I flatter myself it will appear rent and torn only with respect to certain strings of connection and allusions bearing a reference to other matters of my production, which I keep still in reserve. Nevertheless it will be expected that I should give some more particular account of my dealing out this piece of a performance, than barely the allowableness of so doing, after the example of other people.

The *Searches*, from whom I claim to be descended, were a very ancient family, as old almost as the time when curiosity first began to prevail in the world. But as this quality, while left to follow its natural bent, would catch indifferently at every thing novel or engaging, of what kind soever, our line have always endeavoured to confine it to objects from whence something useful might be gathered, either for improving the knowledge or promoting the service of mankind. But as many of us have but moderate capacities, we often labour to little purpose, and fail of producing the good expected from our endeavours; yet we still continue those endeavours, like other Projectors, in hopes of better fuccefs by and by, or for the chance that what little we produce may occafion others to improve upon it, and fo be made to yield better fruits when cultivated by abler hands. But there is one benefit we cannot well fail of, the having employment for our time, together with the foothing fatisfaction of knowing that our aim is juftifiable, and of being engaged perpetually in purfuit of fomething that carries the appearance of ufe and importance. For perfeverance and good intention are characteriftics of the *Searches*, and direct them feverally to thofe courfes of enquiry wherein their particular turn of mind or opportunities render them moft likely to proceed with effect.

It has been my fortune, or my humour, to lay out much of my thoughts upon moral Philofophy, and the rules of Pruduce for the government of our conduct, which I find generally made to confift of detached tenets or maxims varioufly underftood, having little dependance upon each other, but oftentimes appearing to clafh; from whence great difputes and perplexities unavoidably enfue. For men proceed

ceed upon different principles, which they feverally efteem felf-evident, and therefore will not fuffer them to be queftioned. But it feems to me, that many things are received as principles, which are not truly fuch, but deductions from fomething elfe; tho' men efteem them felf-evident, as having forgotten the inducements recommending them to their reception, or having imbibed them from their teachers or companions, without knowing of any other original they ever had. Therefore I conceived it might be expedient to take our principles themfelves under examination, not with defign to overthrow them, for they may be true as conclufions, though not felf-evident as principles, but in order to trace them down to the foundations whereon they ftand. And it foon appeared that human underftanding can build fecurely on no other foundation than experience and obfervation of ourfelves, and that part of nature lying within our cognizance; nor can any abftract reafonings be depended upon which do not ground ultimately upon that bottom.

To the READER.

Under this perfuafion I fet myfelf carefully to confider the nature of the mind, her manner of acting in the common occurrencies of life, the fources of good and evil ordinarily befalling her, what Ideas naturally occur from contemplation of things external, and what conclufions might be drawn from thence for regulating as well our theory as our practice. For I conceived, that if fomething of a fyftem could be formed upon this bafis, it muft carry a mutual dependance in all its parts, which would contribute, fo far as it extended, to render our opinions confiftent and uniform: becaufe our premifes being taken from common experience of things obvious to every body's obfervation, whatever could be plainly deduced from thence muft meet with every body's approbation; and if we could be brought to try our feveral notions by that touchftone, and model them according to that ftandard, it muft tend towards a general reconcilement; an object more fuitable to my tafte than oppofition or victory.

Therefore without interefting myfelf in the difputes which have divided the world,

To the READER.

I endeavoured to ſtrike out what lights I could from experience, without prejudice or partiality, yet with ſuch deference to the opinions of others before me, as to preſume them well grounded, until I ſeemed clearly to diſcern wherein the error lay; and rather deſirous of putting ſuch conſtruction upon them as appeared reaſonable, than forward to reject them.

This attempt has furniſhed me more employment than I imagined at firſt ſetting out; for I found, in the progreſs of my enquiries, that one diſcovery gave birth to another, that to a third, and ſo on to a length I could ſcarce have thought capable of being traced out, much leſs that I ſhould be ſo lucky as to trace it. And I began to fear, that what with unavoidable avocations, what with my natural ſlowneſs, and ſome bodily infirmities rendering me unfit for long and hard labour, the work I have drawn upon my hands, though not likely to prove very voluminous, was more than could be compleated while I have ſtrength and ſpirits to go through it. This made me think of giving out what I had gotten ready, without ſtaying until the whole
were

To the READER.

were finished, had I judged it safe or prudent so to do. But as I have endeavoured all along to proceed with a perfect freedom, and at the same time to avoid a licentiousness or wantonness of thought, my freedom has led me to maintain some positions which might give offence, or be thought of dangerous consequence: and tho' when it shall be seen what use I shall make of them, I trust they will not only be found innocent, but to corroborate those received opinions they seem at first sight to subvert; yet my caution with-holds me from uttering any thing that might appear poisonous, until I had prepared the antidote.

For truths are not to be spoken at all times indiscriminately; because the most useful of them standing sometimes connected in men's minds with error, it would do hurt to undeceive them in the latter, without having provided means of dissolving the connection.

The little Dissertation here presented to view seemed the only part of my productions proper to be ventured abroad alone, as being less complicated than others with the rest, and not so much a new

super-

To the READER.

superstructure raised upon grounds before laid down, which when detached from its foundation might appear like a castle in the air, as a clearing the way for other buildings. For it contains no more than an attempt to rescue the doctrine of universal Providence, as maintained in the preceding chapter, from an objection ordinarily occurring against it, as if it subverted human liberty, by leaving us nothing in our power to do: an attempt which surely cannot give offence to the most scrupulous, whether Divine or Philosopher. And yet I foresee that some exceptionable consequences may be drawn from this doctrine in the latitude whereto it is here extended; but they will probably be overlooked, by those especially whom they might be most likely to stagger; therefore I shall not be so indiscreet as to point them out, until in my further progress I shall have gotten matters ready for obviating them.

It would be departing from the honesty and ingenuousness of the *Searches* to deny, that perhaps the true reason of my exhibiting a part of my face in open view may be no
other

other than an impatience of appearing in print, and reviewing my labours in a fairer character than I can give them with my own scribbling hand. But if this be my motive, it is more than I know myself; for it is not uncommon with every body for imagination to suggest solid and substantial reasons in support of any thing they have a mind to; and such are not wanting, which to my thinking determine me upon the present occasion.

For by submitting this specimen to the judgement of any who shall think it worth his perusal, I may receive some admonitions for my conduct in proceeding further. A man is no competent judge of his own performances; for being the product of his own thoughts, they must tally exactly with his ways of thinking; which upon revisal may give them a face of neatness and proportion they will not carry in the eyes of other people: so that after all his care to make his arguments connected and compact, others may find them abounding in gaps and superfluities; the explanations he gives as clear and full may be thought obscure and imperfect by them; observations

that

that look striking and appofite to him, they may pronounce flat and unavailing; and matters he judges momentous, may to them appear trifling. Nor can one fafely depend upon the judgement of intimates; for however impartial and difcerning they may be, ftill the knowledge of the perfon raifes a curiofity upon what he produces, which will keep up their attention in places where a ftranger might have fallen afleep: befides that there is always fome fimilitude in the way of thinking between perfons who converfe often together. Therefore whatever precautions one may take at home, there is no knowing how one may be received in public without making the trial.

My manner of handling the fubjects I treat of is what I am moft fufpicious of reprehenfion upon; for they being generally unentertaining and dry, I have endeavoured to embellifh them with a diverfity of ftile, in order to relieve the Reader, and keep his attention awake; intermingling fometimes poetical and rhetorical figures; fometimes familiar and vulgar images among abftrufe fpeculations; fometimes giving the reins to a playful fancy in the tranfitions, feverally

intro-

introducing them; and sometimes talking to my Reader as if we were sitting together over a bottle. In these particulars I am willing to stand under correction, as not knowing myself whether all this be an agreeable variety or a motley mixture; whether an ornament setting off the substance, or a disfigurement rendering it hideous.

Whatever information I can pick up, either with respect to matter or form, will not be utterly lost upon me; for though I cannot promise to work a thorough reformation, it being difficult to depart from a track one has long habituated one's self to, and that enthusiasm sometimes possessing a writer not lying always under controul; yet neither am I of a temper to persist obstinately in a fault which I find in my power to mend.

As for gaining applause for my performances, it is what I neither expect nor desire; for the *Searches* were never remarkable for a fondness of fame; the point they constantly drove at was to secure a self-approbation in the justness of their undertakings, and of the measures they took to pursue

To the READER.

purſue them; but being diffident of themſelves, they could never poſſeſs this ſolace compleatly, until they had it confirmed to them by the ſanction of others. I ſhall think it ſufficient encomium, if any body ſhall ſay the ſame of me as *Horace* did of *Lucilius*, that when he run incorrect, yet there was ſomething you would think well worth your while to pick up: and whether this ſomething can be found or no, I ſhall reap an advantage from the diſcovery either way. For if I have been labouring all this while to no purpoſe, it will be expedient for me to know it. I ſhall then be delivered from the fatigue of toiling any longer after an *ignis fatuus*, a mere notion of being important without the reality: I ſhall have more time to ſpare for innocent amuſements, and may enter into them with a quiet conſcience, upon being convinced of an unfitneſs for things uſeful. For I am luckily placed in a ſituation that binds me down to no particular taſk; I may either work or play, as I ſee proper; and my life would paſs more pleaſurably in the latter, could I once lay aſide the thought of obligation to the former. On the other hand, ſhould that

Some-

Something be found in the little sample I deal out, which might prove of service to any body towards clearing up his doubts, or casting a light upon matters he judges of some moment, it will raise a hope and alacrity that will support me under my future labours, and enable me to pursue them more effectually; and may acquit me of some omissions in private life, which seem to call for an excuse.

For my friends and neighbours find it difficult to draw me out of my retirement, or get me to consort among them when near, or correspond with them when distant: which I am apprehensive they may ascribe to an unsociable sullenefs of temper, or a selfish fondness for idle speculations, in disregard of what is owing to persons around me, though they are more polite and good-natured than to charge me openly with these blemishes. Now I have too great a value and desire of their good opinion to rest easy under the thoughts of having forfeited it: therefore am willing to show them that I do not sit idle while retired within myself, assuring them at the same time that I am detained in my hermitage

To the READER.

mitage by something bearing the air of business and obligation, and that it did not appear to me the indulgence of an unsociable humour to be employed in researches after what might prove beneficial to society. But if I should obtain a testimonial from any body who has in anywise received benefit from my speculations, or shall pronounce them worth the pains I have taken in pursuing them, this will avail me more than any protestations of mine; because the best intentions persisted in without producing some good effect, while they justify the heart cast a slur upon the understanding. And least it should be thought that the little I have to shew might be dispatched at leisure hours, without interruption to other engagements; I beg leave to observe, that a great deal more is requisite to be done than appears to such as have not experienced it; for though I have endeavoured as far as in me lies to attain an easy manner of conveying my thoughts, yet we have it upon Mr. *Addison*'s authority, that there is a great difference between easy writing, and what any one may easily write, especially in handling such knotty subjects

To the READER.

subjects as I have fallen upon. I am sure it has cost me infinite pains to save pains to my Reader; and I have been forced to run over in my thoughts as much as would fill ten sheets, before I could furnish out a single one in a manner that might afford a tolerable expectation of being satisfactory to him. Add to this, that the weakness of my spirits disables me from performing great matters at a sitting; but I must do my work by snatches, morning or afternoon, as I find myself in a cue for it: this makes me unwilling to multiply those engagements which take up a great part of the day; for if I am not allowed liberty to catch at every favourable gale as it rises, I shall make no progress in my work, nor can hope to finish it before the time comes wherein I can work no more. It was an old observation, that art is long but life short; and this may be applied to nobody with more truth than to myself, for instead of wanting employment for my time, as is the case with many people, I want time for my employment: therefore I hope my good friends will indulge me in being parsimonious, in consideration of my poverty,

and

and permit me to leave the larger confumptions of it to thofe who have lefs to do, or better fund of ftrength and fpirits to fupport the expence.

The gentle Reader may expect, that in compliance with general cuftom, I fhould befpeak his favourable attention, by expatiating upon the importance and excellence of my fubject; but our family having never yet given into the cuftom, I fhall not begin it now, but leave him to find them out as well as he can; and only prefent him with the defign I have aimed at in all my labours: which is none other than to recommend mutual Good-will to mankind, and a hearty Zeal for one another's benefit. I fuppofe there is nobody who is not willing to promote his own intereft, or would be lefs willing to promote thofe of other people, if it could be fhewn that he ferves himfelf moft effectually by doing his utmoft to ferve them. Now it feems to me not impoffible to make it appear, from the contemplation of nature external and internal, together with certain inferences juftly drawn in order therefrom, that every man's private intereft ftands neceffarily connected with

with the general good, so that whatever advances or hurts the one, must in like manner affect the other: and the dominion of Providence defended in this chapter, is a principal link in the chain employed for that connection.

With respect to the particular part presented in the following sheets, I shall say no more than this, that although Prescience, Fate, and other matters herein contained, are generally esteemed dismal and dangerous subjects, apt to distract the brains of such as have entered deeply into them; and though the natural coldness of my constitution renders me very susceptible of alarms; yet in the manner wherein I have brought them to lie in my thoughts, I see nothing terrifying or gloomy in them, but rather a comfortable prospect in finding that chance and human frailty, which we must acknowledge to have a great influence upon all our proceedings, stand under controul of Wisdom and Goodness. If upon the scene here exhibited, they shall appear to lie in the same manner to the Reader, my purpose is answered: only I beg leave to advertise him, that as I found it no easy

matter

matter to bring them into this train, so he must expect to find some pains and attention requisite in following it; for we shall be unavoidably compelled to spin very fine in some places, and without gentle and cautious usage the thread will break in his hands. Therefore he must not go to work in a hurry; for disquisitions of this sort are not to be run off like a novel, where one has little else to do than to drive on post haste to see how it ends; but he must take care to digest one thing well before he proceeds to another; for here, as in the human body, an error in the first concoction is not to be rectified afterwards. Particularly I would recommend to him to settle well his ideas of Liberty and Freewill in the several lights here represented, and to fix thoroughly in his mind the distinction between the two kinds of Possibility before he goes on to things beyond, which without this caution will scarce appear clear or intelligible. If what he reads should give him scope for further reflection, and put him upon running over the arguments again in his own way, I would wish him to dwell as little as possible upon mere abstractions, but to judge of the abstract in the concrete: and when he has fixed upon particular instances, wherein he conceives either Fate or Freewill to have operated, first to examine each of them singly, and then compare them together, in order to form his general inferences therefrom.

There are some expressions, particularly that in the introductory section, of riding upon the rays, that will appear mysterious: but this must always be the case with the middle of a Composition, wherein things are alluded to with which the Reader has not yet been made acquainted. Therefore he must acknowledge I have acted fairly, by giving him notice in the Title Page, that he was not to expect a Work, but the Fragment of one; for he may choose whether he will meddle with such broken wares or no; but if he does condescend to deal in them, he must not blame me for some little inconveniencies unavoidable in a traffic of this sort.

But those expressions he may look on for the present as excrescencies, not interrupting the chain of reasoning, of which I have

have cut him off a length he may examine by itfelf independantly on the matters alluded to: which whoever will take the trouble to do, fo as to make himfelf mafter of the argument as here purfued, will be qualified to give me his advice thereupon: and if he fhould find himfelf inclined to fay fome civil things of me, I will tell him the grounds upon which I conceive they might be expected. One of the exceptionable pofitions advanced in former chapters, which perhaps may draw both Divine and Philofopher upon my back, is this, that things are not laudable in themfelves, but merit commendation or cenfure, according as either would be moft ufeful; the one being applicable as a fpur, ftimulating men to perfevere in what they have done well; the other as a bridle, reftraining from the repetition of what they had better have let alone. Therefore if my Reader chances to be in the fame way of thinking, he will give me more or lefs encouragement in proportion as he wifhes to fee more of my handy work, or to have any body elfe turn their hand to the like employment.

PREFACE of ANNOTATOR

THE ... audience ...
... ...
some distant ...
...

... that there had one who the fullest esteem, and yet not the least, such
as may be expected among fellows. For
what talents asked upon portion of the
like objects, are apt to begin a rivalship
with majority, but ill companions with perfect steadiness. Now there is this difference
between which wonderfully well adapts
as an instance, to my worthy friend
... Mr. Edward Search. For ...
... an under branch of the
... the like family-turn for
... ... ; but being unable to
... ... of their own, they
delight

PREFACE

OF

The ANNOTATOR.

THEY say similitude conciliates affection; but then it must have some diversity mingled amongst it; as *Ovid* said of the three Ladies, that they all had one and the same set of features, and yet not the same, such as may be expected among sisters. For equal talents turned upon pursuit of the same object, are apt to beget a rivalship and jealousy, but ill compatible with perfect friendship. Now there is this dissimilar similitude which wonderfully well adapts me for an attachment to my worthy friend and relation Mr. *Edward Search*. For the *Comments* are an under branch of the *Searches*, having the like family-turn for the usefully curious; but being unable to strike out any thing of their own, they

delight

delight to rummage among other folks works, examining, comparing, digesting, explaining, illustrating, expatiating, and doing any other little office they think may render them more serviceable. Some of us indeed, to our shame be it spoken, have undertaken things above our pitch, nor spared even the Bible itself; which they have overwhelmed with such a variety of expositions, and found so many contrary senses in the same text, that it is become difficult to see any sense at all, through their envelopements. For my part, I never would attempt any thing of this sort without consulting my Cousin *Search*, who has dropped a hint, that in his next volume he may possibly allow me the liberty, after having prepared some instructions for my conduct. In short, we seem cut out for one another; he pleases me, by furnishing me with matter to spend my thoughts upon, and I please him with the fondness I show for his speculations. So we are grown hugely intimate; we communicate every thing, and know one another as well as we do ourselves; nay, we strive to enter into each others sentiments more carefully than

perhaps

PREFACE *of the* ANNOTATOR. xxvii

perhaps moſt people do into their own: for *Search* has obſerved ſomewhere, that there are many latent deſires and imaginations in the human breaſt unknown even to the owner. 'Twas I, that firſt put him upon this publication: for, good Couſin, ſays I, may not it be expedient to cut off a ſample from the loom before you finiſh your piece, in order to ſhow it about amongſt the Mercers for their opinion of the deſign? This ſeems adviſeable for one who works out of the common track, intermingling figures of the moſt oppoſite caſt among one another. Some people have blended jeſt with topics of Religion, in order to turn them into jeſt; others have conveyed precepts of Morality and common Prudence, in fables, figures, and allegories: but few ſince *Plato* have attempted to interſperſe humour and gaiety among cloſe argumentations, metaphyſical refinements, and diſſertations upon the moſt ſerious ſubjects. Humour and Religion are both very delicate things, and though agreeable in themſelves may ſuffer by their commixture, as tea and ſnuff laid in the ſame drawer ſpoil one another's flavour, nor without

dexterous

dexterous management can they be so joined as that one shall not lose its dignity, nor the other its liveliness. Now you know we have worked all along by ourselves, and how much soever we may have pleased our own fancy, can never know how we shall please others without making the experiment. Troth, Cousin, says he, I believe your advice is good. But what would you have me do? I cannot publish my work imperfect, the design being connected in its several parts; some of which separated from the rest might be liable to misconstruction, and make me thought aiming at conclusions furthest in the world from my intention. I was sensible of this, says I, therefore never pressed you before. But methinks the chapter you have just now finished, contains an entire pattern that may be shown without disgusting the eye for want of other figures to join with it. Perhaps so, says he. But there are many allusions to former chapters, which without being let into the matters alluded to, must appear unintelligible and mysterious. Oh! says I, you don't consider how fond the world is of mysteries. They

PREFACE *of the* ANNOTATOR. xxix

are never so well pleased as with blanks, initial letters, and innuendos, which it may be have no meaning, and therefore cannot possibly be understood. True, says he; yet still they love to have a chink to peep at the mystery, though not enough to unveil it. Why, is it impossible, says I, to have a few chinks opened some how or other by proper Annotations where necessary? He saw my drift, and replied, I am too earnest in running off my principal work to do any such thing. You know I begun late in the day, having employed the former part of my life in laying in a stock of materials, and bringing my thoughts into some regular train. You have sometimes compared me to the silkworm, that devours voraciously for a while, and then applies wholly to the business of spinning herself out. My day is far spent, and I have a long web to spin, which I fear I shall scarce be able to compleat before night; especially as there are some of my brother worms, who being no spinsters themselves, delight perpetually to crawl over me and interrupt my work: so I must not stop to revise, remark, or explain.

explain. But if you have a mind to undertake the job, I shall take it kindly. You know the particulars alluded to, as well as I myself; and have leave to open the chinks as wide as you judge proper. With all my heart, says I. But that I may not exceed my commission, let me know the extent of it. As you say you run off your work without revising, I may chance to find something obscure or liable to be misunderstood, or omitted in an argument that might have been pursued further; may I supply what you seem to have forgot? By all means, says he. And you will probably find room enough for this substituting office: for the state of my brain corresponds but too much with that of the weather: so where you perceive the effect of eastern chills, you may do me good service, by suggesting what I should have done had the air been milder. We have lived long enough together in intimacy for you to know all my thoughts, and may use your discretion upon them. Have a care, says I, what you do. It may be dangerous to give me an unreserved liberty with all your thoughts. What if I should happen

PREFACE *of the* ANNOTATOR. xxxi

happen to touch upon some of the peculiarities in them? You have so long accustomed me to a habit of Sincerity and Plaindealing, I shall not know how to palliate or cover them over with plausible colourings. No matter for that, says he, I desire no colourings. I know you are an honest fellow, and will not do me an injury by misrepresenting me. Only take care not to throw out what might do hurt to squeamish palates. If you do not offend other people, you cannot offend me.

So having obtained full permission, I went to work upon a lining for his brocade; which he being pleased to say was not unsuitable to the pattern he had cut off, we resolved to push them both out upon the shop-window: wholly uncertain how they might take with the passengers, any further than as it will probably be said, They are an Original.

CUTHBERT COMMENT.

From my Apartment in
Search-Hall, 4th *October*,
1762.

ERRATA

Pag. 40. l. 19. *for* forborne *read* forborn
    102. l. 13. *for* gout to, which *read* gout, to which
    124. l. 20. *for* it is my option, and I know *read* it is in my option, and know
    174. l. 15. *for* proceedings *read* proceeding
    188. l. 9. *for* refiftable *read* refiftible
    265. l. 22. *for* volocity *read* velocity
    ult. l. ult. *for* ferve *read* fervice

CHAP. XXIV.[a]

FREEWILL, FOREKNOWLEDGE, and FATE.

SECT. I.

BEHOLD us now arrived at the moſt intricate part of our journey, an impracticable wilderneſs, puzzled with mazes, and perplext with errors, where many mighty have fallen, and many ſagacious loſt their way; for ſhadows, clouds and darkneſs cover it; or what flaſhes of light break out from time to time, preſent the image of truth on oppoſite ſides, the winding paths lead round the diſappointed travel-

Tranſition.

---

[a] The Reader is not to conclude from the high number of this chapter, that the Author has huge piles of his labours in ſtore: for there is but one more chapter ſo long as this, and many of them will run off in ſeven or eight pages.

Transition.

traveller to the spot from whence he set out, or involve him in difficulties wherein neither Protestant nor Papist, neither Divine nor Philosopher has yet found an opening, and which the sacred muse of *Milton* pronounced insuperable, even by the Devil himself.

In this dangerous road we may be allowed with better reason than the Poets, to call in some superior power to our aid; but what Muse, what Spirit, what God shall we invoke? For here are no private transactions unseen by mortal eye, no dreams of *Rhesus* broken off by the sleep of death, no secrets of nature lying beyond our reach to be discovered: we need not dive into the bowels of the earth, nor ascend to mix among the dances of the planets, nor dissect the human frame to find all the curious threads of its organization. But our business lies with the common actions of life, familiar to every one's and every day's experience: we want only to know, whether a man may act freely who makes his choice upon motives suggested by external objects, whe-

ther

Transition.

ther he may know beforehand what his neighbour will do, or offer inducements which will infallibly prevail on him to one particular manner of behaviour, without infringing upon his liberty. Questions that one would think could scarce admit of a dispute; nor do they with common understandings, until men of uncommon refinements have, by their abstractions, spun them into a sense not naturally belonging to them, and introduced a confusion into their ideas, by an inaccuracy of language. Therefore upon this subject I conceive we shall have more to do with words than with things, nor find so much difficulty in ascertaining the facts to be taken under consideration, as the proper import of the expressions employed in speaking of them.

Come then thou solemn power Philology, pioneer of the abstruse Sciences, to prepare the way for their passage, enwrap me in thy close-bodied leathern jacket, that I may creep through the brakes and brambles of equivocation without their catching hold

Transition.

of me; lend me thy needle-pointed pencil, that I may trace out the hair-breadth differences of language; assist me with thy microscope to discern the minute changes of ideas passing to and fro among the same words, as they change their places in different phrases.

If any one will follow me while I travel under thy guidance, let him look for other-guised entertainment than when bestriding Pegasus [a] we bounded along the rapid rays of solar or stellar light, to visit the *Athenian* [b] and *Samian* [c] Sages, to behold the

---

[a] The Author some time ago was favoured with a Vision, wherein he was rapt in extacy out of his body, and transported to the intermediate state lying between death, and the final consummation of all things; where he saw surprizing things not yet lawful to be uttered. Pegasus is only a figurative term to express the flights of imagination: for the Author did not ride upon a flying horse, but was dragged along by one of the old inhabitants, who was expert in walking upon such moveable ground as the rays of light.

[b] *Plato* and *Socrates*, with whom the Author conversed in his excursion.

[c] *Pythagoras*, from whom he received a very scientific lecture, containing many curious matters, partly orthodox, and partly heretical.

Transition.

the wonders of the vehicular state [d], and boundless glories of the mundane soul [e].

For thou, Goddess, consortest not with the Muses nor the Genii, the flights of imagination affright thee: figure and ornament are thy abhorrence, for they blend together in wanton assemblages those ideas which thou art most sollicitous to keep asunder: familiar example [f] alone, of all the flowery train, thou admittest to shed his lustre upon the print of thy mincing

[d] Inhabited by *Woolaston*'s vehicles, that is, departed souls, carrying with them an inner tunicle, or fine organization of corporeal substance, inconceivably small, but infinitely more active and lithsome than our gross bodies.

[e] A created Being, of unlimited power, understanding and excellence, commensurate with the universe, whereinto the spirits of men are absorbed on their departure from the vehicular state.

[f] This sprightly Gentleman has proved very serviceable to our Author, who is fond of his company as often as he can get it; as will appear by the sequel: for he has a marvellous knack at opening the passages through briars, rendering abstractions visible, and fixing them upon the memory. It is recommended to all dealers in profound speculations to take his assistance; for he is a younger son of Experience, employed in dispensing his father's stores upon particular occasions as wanted.

feet,

Tranſition,

feet, and render the marks of them more eaſily diſcernible to the ſtraining eye. But induſtry, and ſcrupulous exactneſs, are thy conſtant companions; labour and vigilance thy delight, thorns and briars the favourite plants of thy garden. Whoever undertakes to accompany thee there muſt prepare himſelf for toil and attention; he muſt obſerve the path exactly in which thou leadeſt him, mark all the outlets on either hand, paſs and repaſs the whole length again and again before he ventures into another turning, that he may fix ſo perfect an idea of it upon his memory, as never to miſtake another ſimilar alley for the ſame.

But ſay, Goddeſs, by what avenue ſhall we enter the wildernefs? Does not thy methodical prudence direct, that upon every queſtion we ſhould firſt know preciſely the terms concerning which the queſtion is propoſed? Where then can we better begin an enquiry into the Freedom of Action, than by aſcertaining the proper import of Freedom?

2. Liberty,

Liberty. 7

§. 2. Liberty, says Mr. *Locke*, is a power, and so is will; therefore they cannot be predicated of one another, for it would be absurd to affirm of a power that it has a power. But with submission to the authority of so great a Master, I conceive Liberty a more complex term than he has made it, and though it includes an idea of power, it contains other ideas beside. And as I apprehend it, to be a negative term, implying no more than a denial of restraint and force; for when we say a man is free, we mean nothing else than that there is no hindrance against his doing or forbearing what he has a mind; therefore it will be expedient to consider how we come by the notion of Restraint or Force.

We find ourselves possessed of several powers of action, we can walk, or speak, or think, or can let them alone: sometimes diseases or other accidents deprive us of our powers, and then we can no longer perform the functions of them; but at other times, though we remain possessed of our powers entire, yet we cannot exert them,

them, by reason of something stronger counteracting them. Thus a man in the stocks has not lost his power of walking, the vigour of his muscles is not abated, nor is he less able to bear the fatigue of a journey on foot than he was before; nevertheless, he cannot walk at all, because the closeness of the wood resists the motion of his legs, therefore he is under a restraint which hinders him from using the power nature has given him. So if he be pushed along by another stronger than himself, he must move forward whether he will or no, not that he has lost the natural command of his limbs to put them in motion or keep them at rest; but because he is under a force greater than he can resist.

Thus Restraint is a comparison between some power and an impediment preventing it from performing its proper function, as Force is the like comparison between the power of forbearance, and some external impulse which renders action necessary, but forbearance impracticable; and Liberty denotes the absence of the other two; for when

Liberty.

when we pronounce a man free, we understand thereby that there is nothing either impelling him to do what he would not, or restraining him from doing what he would. So that all three include the idea of Power, Restraint and Force, as well as Liberty, nor can either of them subsist where there is none; for the bars of a prison are no restraint to a paralytic, nor will you give him liberty by unlocking them, neither can you force a man to fly, or a horse to speak.

We may observe further, that Liberty is so far from being the same thing with Power, that it may be restored by the loss, and lessened by the accession of it. Were an act of parliament made to prohibit me from going out of *London* for a twelvemonth, I should think it a grievous restraint upon my liberty; but should I be rendered unable to stir abroad by gout or palsy, or some other complaint which I could not hope to get rid of in the time, the restriction would no longer be such to me, and I should remain as much at liberty, as if the statute
had

had never been made*. On the other hand our cloaths are made to fit our bodies, so that we can move all our limbs freely, notwithstanding the many ligatures and coverings wherewith we are enveloped; but should it please God to cause a pair of wings to sprout out from our sides, we should find our cloaths a troublesome restraint upon us,

* If it be said the law extends to every body without exception, so that women and children are bound by the game acts, as well as the unqualified sportsman, I shall observe, that it is proper the law should speak in general terms, because it would be troublesome to distinguish constantly between the able, and the unable; and entirely needless, the restraint being barely nominal with respect to the latter. And so it would appear, if a law were to be made against what no man can do. As ready as we are to cavil at the ministers, if one of them were to procure an act to pass, laying a grievous penalty upon any who should fly about in the air; however we might suspect his intellects, we should never suspect his having designs upon our liberty, nor grumble at the restriction, which we should see was not a real one. Indeed I have heard the Test Act complained of as a hardship, by such as had no chance of ever rising to preferment; but this is, because they think it disagreeable to have a mark of distinction set upon them: and so is every thing disagreeable that shows a dislike, although we sustain no immediate damage by it.

Liberty.

us, and we muſt ſend for our taylors to cut ſlits in them for letting out the wings, in order to reſtore us that liberty we had loſt by the ſuperaddition of a new power.

Hence we ſee that liberty is ſo far from being inapplicable to power, that it is properly applicable to nothing elſe; nor is it an abſurd queſtion to aſk, whether a power be free, for it implies no more than to enquire how ſuch power ſtands circumſtanced with regard to any force or impediment which might compell or obſtruct the exertion of it. And when we apply ſuch queſtions to the agent, they bear a reference always to ſome power he poſſeſſes, therefore a man may be free and reſtrained at the ſame time with reſpect to different powers of action; for he that is locked faſt in a room may be free to think or ſpeak, though he is not to go abroad; but a power to do ſome particular act cannot be free while conſtrained, nor the contrary.

Indeed there are degrees of freedom, not incompatible with a partial reſtraint, but rather implying it, as when we find ſome
impediment

impediment obstructing us; though not so great as that we cannot surmount it; for a man with heavy jack-boots on can still walk, though not so freely and alertly as in a neat pair of shoes: such obstacles do not debar us the use of our powers, but render it difficult and laborious, or limit them in compass.

§. 3. Let us now cast back our eye upon the path we have trod, in order to discover what equivocal outlets there may be to mislead the unwary traveller. We get our idea of power, says Mr. *Locke*, from the changes we see made in substances by one another: therefore the word Power originally and properly denotes a quality or property in something to cause those changes, and is synonimous with ability, and we have hitherto used it in that sense. But it often carries a larger signification, comprehending other circumstances besides ability; so that according to the various lights wherein we place it, a man may have power when he has it not; that is, he may

Liberty.

may have it in one sense while he wants it in another.

Suppose a person of full health and vigour bound down in his bed by a multitude of threads wound all over him; another seeing him lie motionless, but not knowing the occasion, fancies him struck with some sudden distemper that has taken away the use of his limbs; he laments his unhappy condition, in being at once deprived of all his powers of action: must not we pronounce this complainant mistaken, for that the man has lost none of his powers, but they all remain entire as ever, though he cannot use them until the strings that tie him down be loosened? If a second person comes into the room who takes the case differently, ascribing the man's inactivity to a fit of laziness with which he upbraids him, shall we not plead in his excuse, that it is no fault of his that he does not rise, for that the bandages hold him down so tight, he has no power to stir either hand or foot?

Thus

Thus we see that power may be truly affirmed or denied in the same instance, according to the manner wherein the question is proposed, or thoughts of the person proposing it; and a man may have ability sufficient for performing a work, which yet he is not able to do, by reason of some obstacle, want of some instrument or material, or other circumstance standing in the way.

We may presume Mr. *Locke* understood Power in this extensive latitude, when he made it the same with Liberty; for where he observes that a man on the south side of a prison has power to walk northwards but not southwards, this were not true, if spoken of natural ability; for the same vigour of limbs which might carry him one way, would suffice to carry him any other; therefore if he want power to walk southwards because the walls of the prison obstruct his passage, the term must be so construed as to include Liberty; and in this sense it would indeed be as absurd to ask,
whether

Liberty.

whether a Power be free, as whether Blueness be blue, or Hardness hard.

§. 4. We may remark further, that Knowledge is often confounded with Power; for ideal causes* being requisite to direct us in the choice of proper actions, we can no more proceed without them than we can without ability. If I have a paper in my custody which I have mislaid, upon being urged

---

* The Author has a chapter upon these, and makes them a species of ideas, as he does motives, or final causes, an under species of them. The distinction between these three may be explained by the following instance. A man walking in the fields may see birds flying, or cattle grazing, which strike ideas upon him, but such as are no causes of any thing he does; for he would walk in the same manner if they did not appear. The sight of his path, together with the windings and turnings of it, and his remembrance or information of the right way, where it parts into two, are ideal causes without which he could not proceed; for if he had them not, he might stumble against a stone, or wander out of the way. But health, business, or diversion, are final causes; because without these, or some other purpose in view, he would not walk at all. Thus ideal causes are that part of our knowledge, which does not instigate us to action, but directs us how to shape it.

urged to produce it instantly, I shall be apt to alledge that it is out of my power so to do, not because I have not the key of the drawer where it lies, nor strength in my fingers to take it out as well as any other paper, but because I know not where to look for it. So if a countryman wants to speak with a person living at the further end of the town, he may say it is out of his power to find the house; not that he wants pliancy in his joints to carry him through all the turnings leading thither as well as any citizen, but because he should lose his way for want of knowing the right. But this idea does not enter into disputes concerning freedom, for ignorance is esteemed a defect of power rather than an abridgement of liberty.

It has been shewn in Chap. II. that what we generally call an Action [b], is not one, but a series of many actions; and when we go about to do a thing, we proceed to

---

[b] And it is expedient for common use that we should call it so; for were we to enumerate all the minute motions we make upon every occasion, we should

to the accomplishment of it by several intermediate steps, each whereof requires a particular exertion of power to perform it. Now if there stand an impediment any where in the way, we cannot do the thing proposed; nevertheless we remain still at liberty to take the steps lying on this side the impediment, and at all events can use our endeavours, how ineffectual soever they may prove. Thus if a man be hindered from going to *London* by floods out in the road, he may yet go up to the edge of the flood without obstacle: if he be locked into a room, he may push against the door; and if his fingers be bound round with a packthread, he may try to expand them, being at full liberty to give his muscles the inflation proper for spreading them open.

It is observable likewise, that restraint is often confounded with impotence, nor can we easily avoid doing so; for restraint should make no dispatch in our conversations with one another. But when we go to examine the nature of the mind, and scrutinize her manner of proceeding, we shall often find it necessary to analyze action into its constituent parts.

C being

Liberty.

being a comparison between our powers and any thing that might obstruct their exercise, may cease upon their increase, or may be generated by a diminution of our powers, rendering that an obstacle to our motions which was none before. Thus *Sampson*, after being shorn of his strength, was brought under confinement by the same cords which were no infringement of his liberty aforetime, and if they had remained on him until his hair had grown again, he would have been restored to liberty by the return of his strength, without any alteration in the strength of the bandage.

Therefore we pronounce upon the same case, as being a defect of power or of liberty, according to the light wherein we place it: the laws prohibiting the alienation of church lands, are called sometimes disabling, and sometimes restraining statutes; and we speak indifferently of a man being disabled to go abroad or confined at home by a distemper. But in strictness, the beginning of a fever works no disability, for

Liberty. 19

for there is generally then an unusual strength and flow of spirits, so that the patient might do as he did at other times, if it were not for the necessary regard to his health, which is a bar against his stirring out of the house; whereas a palsy does ⬛ properly confine, for air and exercise might be wholesome, and nothing hinders you from going abroad, but you are not able, the use of your limbs being suspended by the distemper.

Mr. *Locke* says, that active power belongs only to spirit: however this be, we certainly conceive it, and in our common discourses speak of it as residing in things inanimate; therefore we apply the terms Force and Restraint when we perceive them acting or moving in a manner different to that we should expect from their natural properties, as we do Liberty, when nothing hinders their operations: we talk of a free air, a pendulum swinging, or a river running freely, where there is no obstruction against their motions; of water being forced upwards by an engine, or a stream confined within its channel, by raising the banks.

Hence it appears, that the force of inertness ascribed by Naturalists to matter, and the force of impulse causing its changes of state from motion or rest to the contrary, does not carry precisely the same signification with force in vulgar language; for 'tis the impulse of gravitation, together with its own inertness, or perseverance in a motion once received, that makes a torrent rush violently into the sea; yet every common man apprehends water to run downwards of itself, nor ever esteems it under a force, unless when he sees it driven upwards by some other power, nor under restraint, unless when something obstructs the course it would naturally take. And though we talk frequently of the force of a torrent, we do not understand thereby any force the water itself lies under, but that we suppose it able to put upon whatever may happen to stand in its way.

Whoever will examine the language of mankind, may find that we apply expressions

sions to bodies which belong properly to our own manner of proceeding; and how well soever we know the contrary, speak of them as voluntary agents, exercising powers of their own: thus it is said the wind bloweth where it listeth, and we conceive water as having a fluidity or perpetual motion among its particles, unless bound up by a piercing frost.

Nor do the learned abstain from the like catachresis, when they talk of the tendencies and nitencies, the *conatus recedendi* of bodies, the spontaneous or automatic motions of clock-work, or the laws [c] of matter; and even when they abstract from the secondary properties resulting from composition, they seem to conceive rest as the natural state and choice of body which it exerts its power to preserve itself in, as one may gather from their calling the *momentum* or quantity of motion in any body a force, which conveys an idea similar to

[c] For in strictness, law is applicable only to intelligent agents, with-held from using their powers by the fear of punishment, or obligation to authority.

that of a man carried along againſt his inclination by ſome impulſe he ſtrives in vain to refiſt.

§. 5. I take notice of theſe niceties, not ſo much for any benefit they may be of towards determining the preſent queſtion, as for a caution to beware of letting ſuch variations of language lead us aſtray: for the proper and genuine ſignification of freedom being the abſence of all obſtruction which might thwart us in the exerciſe of any power we poſſeſs, we are free when upon employing our power it will take effect; but under reſtraint, when ſomething impedes us in the exerciſe of our power, ſo as that although we ſhould exert it, the proper conſequence of ſuch exertion would not follow.

Thus a man is at liberty to walk, if upon uſing his legs they will carry him to the place he purpoſes; but if there ſtand any wall or bar in the way, ſo that with his utmoſt endeavours he cannot move forwards, then he is not at liberty. And
ſo

Liberty.

so in all actions we have ability to perform, if they would not enſue upon our efforts, it muſt be owing to ſome hindrance which cramps and prevents them from taking effect.

From hence it appears, that Freedom relates to the event of our endeavours, not to the cauſes of them; for whether any or no inducement prevails on me to walk, I am equally free, provided nothing hinders me from walking, if I ſtand ſo inclined; for Liberty does not depend on any thing prior to the exerciſe of my power, but upon what would or would not ſtand in the way after having exerted it, and therefore is not inconſiſtent with any antecedent cauſes or diſpoſition of Providence influencing me to walk; for how much ſoever they may impell me to go out of the room, I am not at liberty to do it while the door is locked, and when the door is opened I am ſet at liberty, how much ſoever they may with-hold me from uſing it.

But it will be ſaid, all this may be very true, and yet affects not the caſe under consideration, as it relates only to freedom of action, concerning which there is no controversy, not to freedom of will: for no *Arminian* will doubt a man's being debarred of his Liberty by shutting him up in a goal; nor will the most rigid *Calvinist* deny, that upon being let loose he is at liberty to go which way he pleases. So the dispute turns, not upon our freedom to do as we will, but upon our freedom to choose out of several actions in our power: and both seem to agree, that whatever act is contained in the plan of Providence must be performed, nor can we will the contrary if we would.

Various Wills.

§. 6. Before we enter upon the discussion of this question, it will be necessary to understand ourselves in the proposing it; for men seem to me not always very clear in their idea of the term Will, as it stands in either branch of the sentence.

We learn, upon Mr. *Locke*'s authority, that we are capable of no more than one determination of the Will at once, and

Various Wills.

whoever observes the motions of the human mind will find her volitions transient and momentary; she varies her action perpetually, willing this instant what she rejects the next; and if she perseveres for a time in one purpose, it is by a train of numerically distinct, tho' similar and correspondent volitions: therefore to ask, whether we can will this present instant, if we will this present instant, would be an idle and trifling question; it must indeed be answered in the affirmative, and so must every other of the like sort; for I can walk if I walk, ride if I ride, or do any thing else you can name, if I do it; and such hypothetical affirmations may be true of things which categorically proposed were absolutely impossible; for it is as true, that I can lift the house if I lift it, or jump over the moon if I jump over it, as that I can take up a pin if I take it up: such propositions are merely identical, making a shew of something profound, but adding nothing to our information.

Therefore

Therefore the question, to mean any thing, must relate to different Times or different Wills, and the drift of it be to enquire either, whether by willing a thing now I can cause myself to will it by and by; or whether if I happen to will opposite things at the same time, as to buy a costly trinket and to save my money, I can by one Will controul the other, or by a third Will choose which of the two shall have the guidance of my conduct.

To the first of these enquiries, one cannot give a direct answer, it being notorious by every day's experience, that we do determine upon what we will do beforehand, and many times do it accordingly, but at other times do it not, and that upon two accounts; either because we have changed our mind, or because though we continue in the same, we find some desire, or terror, or difficulty rise upon us too strong for our resolution; but changes of mind create no doubts concerning liberty; for nobody imagines that our resolving upon a thing lays us under a necessity of performing it,

although

although good reasons should occur to the contrary, or our judgement should alter; nor will deny, that how strongly soever I have determined to leave *London* seven years hence, I may remain perfectly free all the while to determine otherwise whenever I think proper.

Which by the way shews Liberty not incongruous with prior causes; for if I do something because I had resolved upon it beforehand, and this we practise every day of our lives, the volition whereby I perform it must be acknowledged an effect of my former determination, nevertheless will be counted a free act in every body's estimation, provided nothing hinders but that I might omit it; therefore if my first determination were contained within the plan of Providence, the performance may make a part of that plan without infringement of my liberty; for even supposing me influenced to resolve by some irresistible grace, or supernatural impulse, though I was not free in making, I am yet free in keeping the resolution, nor does there need any
more

more than to keep off all suggestions which might alter my judgement, or temptations which might overpower it, and I shall execute what was resolved on by virtue of the freedom remaining within me.

But when we change our conduct without changing our mind, and do not prosecute what we have in our intention, by reason of some appetite drawing the contrary way, then disputes and difficulties arise; because we conceive our Will still exerting itself, but prevented from taking effect by a superior force or impediment counter-acting it, which presents the genuine idea of a want of Liberty.

Thus this question, whether by our present Will we may determine what we shall will at some future time, becomes reduced into that other, whether one Will may controul or confine another coexistent Will.

§. 7. And no wonder we find perplexities in examining metaphysically a question, the terms whereof have no place in the metaphysical vocabulary; for there is a
philo-

philofophical, and there is a vulgar language, and if ftudious men will mingle their abftractions among vulgar ideas, they muft unavoidably bewilder themfelves in mazes and darknefs.

The notion of a diverfity of Wills is unknown to him that carefully ftudies the motions of the human mind, for her acts are inftantaneous and tranfitory; nor can fhe perform any more than one at the fame time: we have various powers of action, and they all lie under the command of the mind to turn them upon one particular object; her giving them that turn is properly volition, and it is as abfurd to imagine fhe fhould exert oppofite volitions together, as that the wind fhould blow eaft and weft.

We may be reftrained in the ufe of our powers, becaufe their operation paffes through feveral ftages; we work upon certain unknown nerves, they inflate the mufcles, the mufcles pull the tendons, the tendons move the limbs, and if there be an obftruction any where, we have not liberty to perform the action intended, how

much

much soever we may endeavour it; but the acts of the mind upon the first corporeal fibre receiving her impulse are immediate, so there is no room for any impediment to interfere in stopping their progress: we may indeed imagine her to lose her power by the fibre becoming incapable, or being removed out of her reach; but we have seen that when power is gone, there is no place either for Liberty or Restraint.

Nor let it be asked, whether the mind be free to determine her own acts; for this implies, that one volition is the consequence of another, and so it may be remotely; but we have shown in a former place, that the mind never acts upon herself, unless by the mediation of motives; for there is no one action of our lives which we do not enter upon through some motive of judgement or inclination, or present fancy; and even if we had an elective power besides our active, how much soever that might determine the latter, it must
itself

itself be determined by some satisfaction apprehended in the choice [a].

But the suggestion of motives to our thoughts is as much an action, as the moving of our limbs, and if any thing obstructs their rising, notwithstanding our endeavours to call them up, we may be free or restrained with respect to that action; but in respect to our first endeavours, we are no more capable of either, in one case than the other [b].

There-

[a] There is a long chapter upon this head, wherein it is endeavoured to overthrow the doctrine of a Free-will of indifference, and to shew, in confirmation of what Mr. *Locke* had advanced before, that the expectation of present satisfaction, or escape of present uneasiness, is the thing that determines the Will in her every motion; that remote good never moves her, unless by the satisfaction taken in making advances towards it; and that when we do wrong, we are misled by present gratification appearing more satisfactory than a greater distant good.

[b] It having been shown in a former place, that the mind never acts upon herself, unless by mediation of some material organ employed to raise ideas of reflection before her; which is an action as much as holding up a paper to exhibit the writing thereon to our sight. Now the mind cannot be restrained from
touching

Therefore we may agree with Mr. *Locke* in pronouncing Liberty as little applicable to Volition, taken in the philosophical sense, as Squareness is to Virtue, or Swiftness to Sleep.

§. 8. But if we listen to the common discourses of mankind, we shall find them speaking of several Wills, several agents in the same person resisting, counteracting, overpowering and controuling one another: hence the so usual expressions of the spiritual and carnal Wills, of the man and of the beast, of self-will and reason, of denying our Wills, subduing our passions, or being enslaved by them, of acting unwillingly or against our will, and the like: all which take rise from a metonyme of the cause for

touching the organ, though the latter may be hindered by some obstacle from answering the touch. Thus if I am prevented from thinking, either by the fumes of indigestion, or the noise of people gabbling about my ears, yet nothing prevents me from trying, which is all the mind has to do; but in one case the organs are rendered unfit to perform their office; and in the other, the ideas they cast up are obscured by those thrown in forcibly by the senses.

Various Wills.

the effect, for our actions being constantly determined either by the decisions of our judgement, or follicitations of our desires, we mistake them for the Will itself: nor is it a little confirmation of the Will being actuated by motives, to find them so intimately connected therewith that a common eye cannot distinguish them apart.

When in our sober moods we deliberate and afterwards fix upon our measures of conduct; we look upon such determination as our Will, which we conceive not a transient act, but an abiding power, exerting itself from time to time as opportunities offer, until either the design be compleated, or fresh reasons prevail on us to alter it.

But it often happens, that some inordinate passion or inveterate habit comes athwart our way, and puts us by from the prosecution of our design, without making us change it: this we likewise regard as our Will, being sensible that what we do by its instigation is still our own act, and because we find the same desire prompting us us at different times, we apprehend this too a permanent power lying in us, ready to be exerted upon the proper objects presenting. Thus we get the idea of two Wills opposing, impeding, restraining, and mastering one another.

Sometimes there ensues a contest between them, the mind hovering uncertain for a while, until at last she settles on either side: hence comes the idea of a third Will, determining between the other two; and I believe this gave rise to the notion of an elective, besides our active power.

But these struggles are owing to the fluctuations of strength in our motives, and the victory to some one of them catching the idea of Satisfaction away from the rest: for 'tis well known, that motives as well of reason as passion, do not always appear in equal colours, nor press with equal force, but urge vehemently or feebly by turns, with frequent and sudden variations: and we may perceive the like wavering in our coolest deliberations between two measures of conduct or two diverfions, wherein the mind cannot be fufpected of giving a preference, being difpofed all along to follow whichever fhall be found the beft or moft entertaining; but both appear fuch alternately, until at laft the ballance of judgement or fancy fettles without intervention of the Will to caft it either way.

§. 9. Neverthelefs, men cannot be put out of their accuftomed manner of talking and thinking, therefore in compliance with their conceptions, let us fuppofe a diverfity of Wills, that thofe Wills exert permanent acts, lafting for hours and days without intermiffion, and that we may will at one time, what we fhall will at another. In this light there is certainly room for applying reftraint and freedom to the Will; for its operations being now conceived paffing through a length of time before they take effect, may be obftructed, or turned afide in their paffage by fomething elfe: fo if I do in the afternoon what I had determined in the morning to forbear, my former Will
ftill

still continuing the same, I am under a force, and the Will I have at present is a different Will from that remaining with me from the morning's determination, and counteracts it.

But it being obvious that we can exert our power only one way at a time, we are apt to entertain a contradictory notion that, while we have a diversity of Wills within us, one of them only is our own, and esteem each of them such in turn according as we chance to be in the humour. Sometimes it is the will of inclination, and must be so taken in all expressions relating to self-denial, to curbing our Wills, or to things we do unwillingly, or against our will, that is, against our liking: but more commonly we understand the determination of our judgement to be our Will, because there are none of us without this Will, for I suppose nobody ever refuses to do what his present judgement represents as best, provided it give him no trouble in the performance, nor thwart any inclination, or fancy whatever, therefore this is a Will always

always subsisting in us, though not always taking effect.

As to the third Will, that of Election, this takes place only occasionally, when there is a contest between the other two: for as nobody ever chooses to act against his judgement without some inclination drawing him, or uneasiness driving him the other way; so likewise I imagine nobody ever chooses to abstain from doing what he likes, when he sees no reason in the world why he should forbear; when Reason and Inclination urge the same way, or one alone sollicits, the other remaining totally silent, which frequently happens, there is but one object presented to the mind, who in that case has no room to make any choice or election at all.

Therefore the will of Judgment or Resolution, in common propriety of language, is to be esteemed our Will, our freedom depending upon the presence, or absence of any impediment which might prevent that from directing our motions: and so St. *Paul* understood it, where he represents the carnal man as omitting to do the things he would, and doing the things he would not, which he juftly ftiles, a wretched bondage: nor can that glorious liberty of the Sons of God, which we are exhorted to affert, be better expounded than by an exemption from all inordinate defires and temptations, fo that we may perform whatever our reafon and duty recommends with eafe and readinefs.

§. 10. But there is a reftraint which our judgement lays upon itfelf, when an action occurs we judge eligible regarded alone, but cannot be done without omitting fomething elfe we judge more expedient, we think ourfelves not at liberty to do it. Thus if I am afked to do fome little good office for a friend, when fome bufinefs of importance calls me another way, I fhall excufe myfelf by faying, I would gladly oblige him if I were not under a neceffity of attending to my bufinefs.

It is this oppofition of things eligible to the judgement, if confidered apart, that gives

gives birth to thofe we have called Motives of Neceffity [a], to Obligation, to Duty, the command of a Superior, the regard for our Health, our Prefervation, the avoidance of Mifchief, or Damage; all which compel us many times to act otherwife than we wifh, or than our judgement would choofe, if thefe bars did not ftand in the way: but this kind of neceffity is a very unftable term, the fame cafe being efteemed fuch in one light which is not in another.

A man having a feal put forcibly into his hand, and the hand with the fame violence preffed down upon wax affixed to a deed, containing a conveyance of his eftate, will be counted by every body under neceffity; but then the fealing is no more his act than it is the act of the feal employed therein,

[a] In a former chapter upon that article, wherein Neceffity is made one of the four claffes under which all our motives of action may be reduced; the other three being Pleafure, Ufe, and Honour. For we never ftir a finger, unlefs to pleafe ourfelves more or lefs, or for fome ufe we apprehend therein, or becaufe we efteem it in fome degree laudable, or becoming, or becaufe we muft for avoiding fome mifchief or inconvenience.

for both act by impulse without any thing that can be called freedom.

But what if his hands being left at liberty, he be only locked up in a room, and threatened to be kept there without victuals or drink until he shall seal? Perhaps he has a wife and children who must be ruined by the loss of his estate, and being a man of resolution, he determines bravely to perish rather than bring them to destruction: in this forlorn condition he lolls out at a window, where he sees an intimate friend of of his, a lawyer, who advises him to execute, for that no damage can ensue therefrom: he then calls for the deed, sets to his seal, and obtains his enlargement. This the Philosopher will not allow to be an act of necessity, for it was in his power to have forborne, and he did actually forbear until his friend's admonition having altered his judgement, he chose voluntarily to seal, upon a prudential motive of saving his life without detriment to his family. The Grantees bring ejectment for the land in *Westminster-hall*, where the whole case appearing

Various Wills.

pearing upon evidence as above, the judge and jury pronounce the deed void, for that the man was under *dureſſe*, and his act not voluntary but impoſed upon him by force. Thus we find the ſame act adjudged neceſſary in legal conſtruction, which was free and voluntary in the philoſophical.

Now to change the caſe a little, imagine the confinement were in a public gaol for a lawful debt, which the party has no means of paying, nor credit to procure bail; ſomebody offers to purchaſe a farm contiguous to his houſe, and which it would be greatly inconvenient for him to part with, nevertheleſs he conſiders his health is infirm, and if he remains in priſon it will inevitably prove his death; ſo he accepts the offer as the only poſſible means of extricating himſelf. If he be afterwards blamed for ſo imprudent a bargain, he will alledge the neceſſity of his affairs compelling him to it; and this allegation will be readily admitted as a full excuſe. If upon ejectment brought, he offers to refund the money, and refuſes to deliver poſſeſſion,

urging

urging the necessity he lay under, I am afraid this plea will not avail him; for the court will say, his act was free and voluntary, nor was he under any compulsion when he did it, therefore it must stand good.

Let us now vary our circumstances once more, and suppose the man under no confinement or debt at all; but he has taken a fancy to some girl of the town; she wants a sum of money to throw away upon an extravagance, and will leave him for some other gallant, unless he will supply her, which he has no means of doing any other way, than by sale of the farm above-mentioned: he is so besotted with her allurements that he cannot live without her; so he executes the conveyance, though sorely against the grain, and against his judgement; he will be apt to plead necessity in excuse for this foolish proceeding; but no indifferent person will admit it for such: here then is a necessity men deem so themselves, though nobody else will call it by that name.

But

Various Wills.

But Neceffity being conftantly oppofed to Freewill, the changeablenefs of thefe terms, according to the lights wherein you regard them, gives rife to as notable difputes among us, as thofe canvaffed of old among the Philofophers concerning the proper colour of the feathers of a cock-pidgeon's neck, which prefents a different afpect upon every little motion of the bird.

§. 11. Every body efteems freedom the bafis of morality; for no man deferves praife or blame for doing what he could not help, or omitting what he was not at liberty to perform: we are juftified in doing things upon the command of a fuperiour, which were blameable had we done them upon our own accord; and it is a received maxim, that neceffity has no law. Neverthelefs the reftraints laid upon us by our vices juftify us not, and the flave of fin is always thought anfwerable for the drudgery he goes through in obedience to his tyrant. On the other hand,

we

we may merit commendation, by complying with the neceſſary obligations of our religion and our duty.

Oftentimes, as has been already remarked, we blend the idea of impotence with want of liberty, or attribute to the one, what proceeds from the other; and indeed the latter in ſome meaſure depends upon the former; for whatever obſtacle ſtands in our way, were our ſtrength increaſed ſo as greatly to ſurmount it, would become none, but we ſhould be ſet at liberty from its oppoſition. A man bound hand and foot with cords, upon having the ſtrength of *Sampſon* given him, would regain his liberty without being untied: and a cobweb wound about our hands makes no abatement in our freedom, though it deſtroys that of a fly; not that it does not oppoſe the ſame reſiſtance againſt our fingers as it does againſt the legs of the fly, but becauſe that reſiſtance is nothing in compariſon with our greater ſtrength.

When ſome fond paſſion captivates the heart, and forces us upon actions our preſent

Various Wills.

sent judgement disapproves, we are said to labour under an impotence of mind; and the compliance with such temptations as few or none can resist, is attributed to the weakness of human nature. When honour, or duty calls a man to some very painful enterprize, like those of *Scævola*, *Regulus*, or the Christian Martyrs, he does not want freedom of action to accomplish it; for his hands will as readily obey the command of the mind to thrust them into burning coals, as into a bason of water, if he can but bring his mind to give the command: perhaps some of us might resolve upon such an exploit, but should probably flinch in the attempt; and we many times do enter confidently upon undertakings where we find our courage fail in the execution: here then is an effect of the Will directing her own volitions, which yet are forcibly turned a contrary way by the terrors of the pain; so then here, if ever, the Will is not free to follow her own choice and election: nevertheless, when

trials

trials of this fort have been undergone; we do not reckon them inftances of greater freewill, but greater ftrength of virtue, and extraordinary vigour of mind.

So if a covetous man intends to give money in charity, but when he comes to take his guineas out of the bag, has not the heart to part with them; he has a will to do a generous deed, and would execute it if not reftrained by his fondnefs for the pelf; yet we do not ordinarily reckon him deftitute of Freewill, but that he has not power to give any thing away. Thus we efteem the fame cafe a defect of Liberty, or of Power, according as we fix our eye upon the ftrength of the obftacle, or feeblenefs of the agent.

Free Agency. §. 12. The Speculative talk much of a free and neceffary Agency, terms not in ufe among the vulgar, nor do they lofe any thing by the want of them: for if we go to examine what Free Agency is, we fhall find it to be no more than the dependency

Free Agency.

dency of actions upon volition *, therefore man is a free Agent, becaufe his limbs move according to the directions of his Will,

* It is not clear that my friend Search has hit the exact notion of free Agency, as underftood by thofe who commonly employ the term. For according to his definition, we muft afcribe it to the Brutes, not excepting the moft ftupid of them, the Slugg and the Beetle; becaufe unlefs we fuppofe them mere *Cartefian* machines, we muft allow their motions to depend upon their volition; for when they crawl to the right hand or the left, it is not by impulfe, like a billiard ball ftruck on either fide, but they are drawn that particular way by fome allurement ftriking their fenfe, and might as well have crawled the contrary, if the like allurement had invited them thither. Yet we do not hold them for free Agents, nor efteem them accountable Creatures, or capable of moral good and evil; as we do man, folely upon account of his having the privilege of free Agency. So that their Agency feems to be of a middle nature, between free and neceffary: fomething that paitakes of both, and yet is neither.

Now in order to fettle the idea of free Agency, let us obferve that man, befides his power of acting according to the motives in his imagination, has a power over the imagination itfelf, to call up ideas there, which would not arife of their own accord. But this power the Brutes feem to want; for though they remember, they do not recollect; they have ideas of reflection, but fuch only as are thrown upon them mechanically; they have combinations and affociations, formed by the frequent appearance of objects together,

without

Will, but Matter a neceſſary Agent, as having no will, and acting ſolely by virtue of the motion or impulſe imparted to it.

Not without any endeavours of their own to unite them; and if they ſometimes make inferences, thoſe are ſuch as occur to them ſpontaneouſly, and are not drawn out by ſtudy and meditation. Now this privilege of voluntary reflection, commonly called Underſtanding or Reaſon, is what denominates us free Agents, and renders us accountable for our manner of uſing it. Not but that in ſome of our actions, one can find no difference from thoſe of our fellow animals: for a dog upon turning the corner of a ſtreet, if he ſaw another dog running againſt him, would ſtart aſide, I ſuppoſe, as well as a man upon the like occaſion. Therefore in this inſtance the actions of both are ſimilar: and numberleſs inſtances might be produced, wherein we act under the guidance of ſenſe and imagination, without direction of our underſtanding, or reflection upon what we are doing. Yet how much ſoever we may act in this manner, without uſing our underſtanding, we might always uſe it if we would: therefore this privilege remaining always with us, we eſteem ourſelves always free Agents: and the omiſſion of uſing it, is equally imputable to us, with any wrong uſe we may make of it.

But to bring off our Author as well as we can, it may be alledged, that thoſe actions only which we perform with a reflex act, or conſciouſneſs accompanying them, and with conſent of the mind upon ſome conſideration, how tranſient ſoever, of what we are about,

Free Agency.

Not but upon a man's being pushed violently down to the ground his fall is necessary, but then it is properly no act of his; for though we are apt to say he hurt himself by

about, are esteemed the work of our will: but what we do inadvertently, by sudden impulse of fancy, or surprize of habit, we are said to do accidentally, or mechanically. Therefore these actions, being ordinarily not reckoned our own, nor effects of our will, it still remains true, that free Agency is the dependance of our actions upon our volition: taking those terms in the sense wherein those who talk of free Agency understand them.

We may observe further, that this double power the human mind possesses, of acting as well upon the imagination as upon the limbs, probably gave rise to the notion of an elective power, coexistent with our active. For her reflex act, introducing new ideas, striking various lights from them, changing the colour of our motives, removing satisfaction to a different point, thereby causing other actions to ensue, than would have followed upon the motives first occurring, and employed as often in adding strength to the follicitations of passion, as weight to the judgements of reason; it is looked upon as the operation of another power, directing that whereby we perform our bodily motions, and setting it at work without the intervention of motives, and even contrary to their influence. Whereas in reality these are not different powers, but one and the same, exercised upon different subjects, to wit, the mental and corporeal organs;

nor

by the fall, which implies something done by him, yet upon mature confideration, we never attribute the hurt to him, but to the perfon who threw him down: for in this cafe his motion is fimilar to that of body, which does not properly act, but only tranfmits the action of fomething elfe that moved it. When a ftone ftrikes againft a wall it ferves only as a channel of conveyance for the force of the engine from whence it was caft, that again of the fprings and wheels whereby it was worked, and fo backwards in a feries of effects and caufes, until you come to fome voluntary agent

nor do they direct one another any otherwife, than as when a man reads an advertifement pofted up againft a market-houfe, the fight of what he reads, raifes a defire he might not otherwife have felt, of purchafing the wares fpecified therein, and directs him where to feek for them; and fo gives birth to other actions than he would have performed upon the motives in his thought, before he turned his eyes upon the paper.

But however this be, it affects not the main argument carried on in the text: for whatever idea we entertain of Agency, ftill our freedom confifts in the removal of all impediment againft it's taking effect upon being exerted, but has no concern at all with the caufes, or inducements prevailing on us to exert it.

giving

Free Agency.

giving the first impulse, whose act it is, whether he intend the consequence or no. If a man shoots another, the wound made by the bullet is his act, and he chargeable with the murder; or if he shot at a crow and happened to kill a man, though he be guilty of no crime, still the slaughter is his act, but an undesigned and accidental one. And if we commonly ascribe powers to body, it is because we cannot trace them back to the causes from whence they originally sprung.

Upon this view of the matter, we see that free Agency has nothing to do with questions concerning Liberty, for the one may remain after the other being taken away. A man shut up in a prison still continues a free agent of such actions as he can perform; if he would gladly go abroad but sits still in his wicker chair, as knowing the doors are locked, his quiescence is an act of free Agency, not like that of the chair he sits on, for he might have rose from it if he would. Or if he be shoved along by the shoulders, though he must move, being under a force, yet he is a free agent in the motion of his legs, for a statue pushed along in like manner, being a necessary agent, would have fallen upon its face.

Thus how much soever we may be abridged or confined in our powers, while there is any thing left that we can do, our free agency subsists entire, for this relates only to our manner of doing those actions we perform, that is, by willing them; and consequently in every thing a man does which is properly his act, whether by compulsion, or restraint, or free choice, he is in that instance a free agent, or in other words, he is such whenever he is an agent at all.

§. 13. But all this will not satisfy the curious, for they ask further, whether a man have free agency to will such a particular exertion of his power as well as to execute it: now this is another kind of Agency from that we have been speaking of hitherto; and for distinction sake we shall beg leave to call it free Volency (for

the

Free Agency.

the Speculative will allow one another to coin a word upon occasion): so the question is not whether man be a free Agent, but a free Volent; for his agency remains the same, provided his actions follow according to his volition, whatever laws this latter be subject to.

Now in order to raise a question upon this head, we must suppose our Volition the effect of some prior or other act of the Will besides the Volition itself under examination: but we have seen in the progress of this work, that the Will is no subject of her own operation, but takes her turns from time to time, according to the present state of the judgement and imagination, therefore the epithet Free, can neither be affirmed, nor denied, nor any ways applied to Volency; this not being immediately produced by any exertion of our power. 'Tis true, we do often determine beforehand what we will do, and pursue measures accordingly, which we should have omitted, had it not been for such determination; and in this sense the Will acts upon herself,

but

but then she does it mediately by fixing such ideas, resolutions, or propensities upon the memory and imagination as will serve her for motives by and by; and it is plain her agency terminates with the impressing such ideas, because if they slip out of our head, or something happens to render the determination inexpedient, though we act contrary to it, yet no doubts arise concerning our free Agency, either in the first determination or subsequent volition.

Besides, some of our actions leave room for no more than one operation of the Will; a man turning the corner of a street sees somebody come hastily against him, and suddenly starts back; here the first act of his Will is that whereby he moves his limbs, so there is no prior Agency whereto the term Free may be applied.

There are some who hold two consubsisting Wills, an active and an elective, the latter continually directing the former, how truly I shall not examine; but upon this supposition man is a free Agent, and a free Volent; for free Agency is the dependance

of

Free Agency.

of his actions upon volition, and free volency the dependance of volition upon his choice; but you cannot go on further to entitle him a free electant too; for I never heard of any body spinning the thread so fine as to suppose another election determining that which determines the Will: all who hold an elective power making it either dependant upon motives, or self-moving independent on all causes whatever, even on any prior, or other act of the Will, so the term Free cannot be applicable to it, because we are free only in such things as will ensue upon some previous act of the Will exerted to produce them.

We do indeed often talk in common conversation of a free, and a forced choice; but this relates to the consequence of our choice, not to the manner of making it, and depends not so much upon our being able to choose, as to obtain the thing chosen. We say indeed, a man has not liberty to choose when he knows the thing is not to be had, because he cannot will an impossibility;

possibility, for how much soever we may wish or desire, we never actually Will without a present apprehension of something feasible: but this proves volition dependant upon final causes, occuring to the imagination, for an unattainable end is no end at all, because it is not a thing wherein our efforts may terminate, nor can the mind raise a volition of it by any power she possesses. Besides that choice, in vulgar acceptation, lies undoubtedly liable to constraint, we meet with numberless instances every day of our being confined in our choice; which shows that choice in this sense is a different thing from the elective power spoken of just now; for that, the maintainers of it insist upon as a privilege inherent in human nature, which nothing can divest us of, nor any external force, or circumstances of situation controul; but that we have always power to will, how much soever we may be restrained from doing.

§. 14. Thus

§. 14. Thus have I endeavoured to point out some of those variations of sense our words are liable to, according to the occasion introducing them, or light wherein they are placed: and it is this fluctuation of language that makes the labyrinth, and throws up the briars and thorns that entangle us in our reasonings upon human Liberty. For men set out with one question, but scarce have gone a few steps before they slide insensibly into another, from thence into a third, and so on without limitation: no wonder then they cannot come to a satisfactory conclusion upon a subject perpetually changing.

I know of no other use [a] in the discussion above attempted of those several changes,

---

[a] Every common man apprehends himself as having the command of his actions, and some understanding to judge of their expedience. He knows his powers are limited in compass, or many times obstructed by outward impediments from taking effect when exerted, and that his judgement is defective. Yet he can always use what judgement he has, and apply his endeavours towards helping himself to the thing it recommends. He sees likewise that there are methods to be

changes, unless to warn men against being beguiled by them, for let them keep their ideas steady, and I believe they will find no difficulties. Therefore I hold it wrong to enter upon a debate concerning free Will in general, that being a variable term, as well in our common discourses, as in our abstract speculations, for the Will is always free,

be employed for improving his judgement, and inculcating motives upon his mind that will invigorate his endeavours in time of action. When he has failed in any of these points, he takes shame to himself for the omission; and when he has done his best, feels an approbation resting upon the deed. All this he can easily comprehend, and is comprehension enough for his use: for in the business of life, we never talk of free Agency, nor find occasion to distinguish between freedom of Action, and freedom of Will, nor to examine how many consubsisting powers we possess, operating upon one another.

Therefore honest Ned acknowledges the fine-spun discussions he has attempted, of no use to such as can be contented to keep within the compass of common sense: but if they will needs launch out into subtile refinements, until they find themselves entangled, he offers his best assistance to extricate them. Only he desires they will not think of untying all the knots at once; but observe where the thread sticks, and apply his directions from time to time, for disingaging it, in that particular part where they find the present difficulty.

Free Will.

free, that is, always doing something or other while we wake, yet at the same time may be confined to one, or a few ways of exerting herself: but let them take into consideration particular acts of the Will, and they will find her sometimes free, sometimes under force or restraint, and sometimes neither of the three applicable to her, according to the different lights wherein they regard the matter, according to what they understand by the term Will, and what they apprehend to be an act of her's.

But with respect to our main point the consistency of human Freedom with Providence, it is not much matter what notions men entertain of Liberty, of Agency, of Will, or Choice, provided they contemplate each instance singly by itself, and do not blend them together, nor change them, by juggling like a conjuror with cups and balls. For they must discern so much similitude in all cases of Liberty that can be produced, if they will but keep their ideas clear, and under such discipline as not to
jostle,

jostle, or run into one another, that the same consequences will always follow, how variously soever they may understand Liberty in the several cases proposed.

§. 15. Let us consider a man just enlarged out of prison, who we shall say has regained his liberty, because he can stay at home, or go abroad this way, or that, north or south as he pleases. So his freedom consists in the dependance of his motions upon his Will, in his standing so circumstanced as that nothing hinders but that rest, or motion, or any particular motion he shall direct, shall ensue upon his willing; it does not at all relate to the inducements he may have for willing, whether some prudential motive, or sudden start of fancy, or impulse of passion, or whether he put it to the cast of a die, in each case he remains at full liberty to do as he will.

Well, but suppose him under the authority of some master, who gives him a holiday to divert himself at home, or go abroad wherever

Free Will.

wherever he chooses. I shall not dispute, whether the injunctions of a Superiour be strictly an abridgement of human Liberty, for that they may be disobeyed by any one who shall disregard the consequences: let us grant for the present, that he could not do the thing whereon his choice shall fall, if any prohibition were given against it, yet there being no such prohibition, leaves him besides his liberty of action, a liberty of choice in what manner he shall use his other liberty: now this liberty, like the former, consists in the dependance of his actions upon his choice; for where he has free choice, nobody can doubt he will do as he chooses; and where he has not, he may be forced to do what he does not choose: but it has no concern with the causes of his choice, whether he spend his holiday prudently, or foolishly, according to his own whims, or the persuasions of an acquaintance.

But suppose he has strong reasons either of religion, or duty, or respect to some Relation who may leave him a good legacy which

Free Will.

which urge him to go one way, but his companions, or his own jovial difpofition, follicit him another to the alehoufe, and nobody has any authority to interpofe, fo he remains ftill at liberty to choofe between them, becaufe he may take either way as his will and his choice fhall direct. No, you fay, 'tis not clear that he has a freedom of choice; for though I admit he may do as he choofes, yet I doubt his being free to choofe; becaufe his evil habit of tippling may force a choice upon him whether he will or no. Beware, my friend, of the mazes in the labyrinth, for we are now ftriking into another alley, and ftarting a different queftion from that we had under contemplation before.

In common ufage, we apply Liberty indifferently to the power or act performed thereby; for we fay the choice is free when nothing hinders, but that we may do whatever it fhall pitch upon, and the act free when it follows in confequence of our choice, and not of any compulfion obliging

Free Will.

ing us to perform it. And one of the moſt dangerous ſources of perplexity ariſes from the want of diſtinguiſhing in our enquiries concerning the freedom of a power, whether we regard it as a cauſe or an effect; for while we behold it in a double light, as too frequently is done, we ſhall never ſee diſtinctly where to find an iſſue. According to your preſent ſtating the doubt, we muſt conſider it as an effect, the proper object of ſome power the man has to influence his choice, unleſs the prevalence of habit ſhould give it a contrary bias.

As to caſes of reſtraint they will conduce nothing to our main purpoſe, therefore we will conſider only ſuch caſes wherein you may ſuppoſe a freedom of choice in our preſent ſenſe of the Term, that is, as an effect of ſome power we poſſeſs.

§. 16. Suppoſe a man deliberating in the morning how he ſhall lay out his afternoon: there are no bolts nor bars in his way, no authority of a ſuperiour, nor reſtraint

straint of law, duty, honour, or obligation intervening in the matters under deliberation, so we know his afternoon's actions will be such as his Will and Choice shall then direct, but neither is there any strong inclination, or passion at work, which might drive him upon one way of employing himself preferably to the rest, so he stands indifferent to choose now in what manner he shall dispose of himself in the afternoon, nor has he any choice until he shall determine it by some present act of his Will.

I do not give this as a philosophical representation of the case, but certain it is, we often do conceive ourselves in a situation (how justly 'tis no matter) to will or choose what we shall will and do by and by [a]: for if

---

[a] But when we act in consequence of a previous choice, we do so, either because retaining in mind the reasons inducing us to make it, or because confiding in our judgement that there were sufficient reasons, or because the expedience constantly found in adhering to a resolution once taken, without which we could compleat none of our purposes, has given us a habit of perse-

Free Will.

if upon afking a friend to walk with you in the Park this afternoon, he fhould gravely reply, Good, Sir, I cannot poffibly tell you, for the prefent moment only is in our power; my future actions depend upon my future volitions, and the Will cannot act upon itfelf, nor is what I fhall do five hours hence the fubject of my prefent option: you would think he bantered you, and be apt to cry, Pr'ythee cannot you choofe either to walk, or let it alone, cannot you tell me whether you will or no?

Therefore unlefs we will talk in a ftrain contrary to the language and conceptions of all mankind, we muft acknowledge that a perfon in the cafe before us has a perfect freedom of choice. But wherein does this freedom confift? where, unlefs in the ab-

---

perfeverance: all which are motives weighing with the Will, unlefs other motives fhould arife to take off their force. Therefore in cafes of prior determination, we operate upon our own Will no otherwife, than we might operate upon the Will of another perfon, by fuggefting motives fufficient to prevail with him; as when we engage a labourer to work for us by the promife of good wages for his fervice.

fence

fence of all impediment, reftraint, authority, obligation or force whatfoever againft his power of choofing, fo that his choice will continue fuch as he fixes it, and his afternoon's actions follow precifely according to his prefent determination, nor has it any thing to do with the motives or caufes inducing him to choofe riding rather than walking, or ftaying at home before both.

But we have not done yet; for fome there be who infift upon an elective Power [b] confubfifting with our power of Volition, and determining it as well in giving the preference to what we are to do

---

[b] *King* upon the origin of Evil, and his Commentator *Law*, place the operation of this elective Power in annexing the idea of Beft, to whatever action we think proper, which then the Will proceeds immediately to perform. Yet they allow the action fo performed to be a free act: which fhews Freedom, even according to their notion of it, not inconfiftent with the influence of motives; for the idea fo annexed, may furely be acknowledged to operate as a motive, influencing the Will to purfue the Action whereto we have united it, as much as if we had found them united by decifion of the judgement, or reprefentation of the fancy.

Free Will.

hereafter, as in the prefent exercife of our bodily powers. Be it fo, fince they will have it fo. Then the freedom of this elective Power depends upon the removal of all force or impediment againſt the Will taking fuch determination as is elected, but not at all upon the caufe of fuch election. Add further, that when we do what we had elected or determined beforehand, nobody will deny our being free in the volitions exerted at the time of execution: which proves Freedom confiftent with Precaufation, for otherwife either our Election and Predetermination muft have no avail nor influence upon our future conduct, or elfe muft put a force upon the Will, conftraining it to act conformably to them until they were compleated.

§. 17. Thus how many powers foever we may conceive in the mind directing one another, the proper and genuine idea of Freedom, with refpect to each of them, will be the fame: for in order to difcufs the point of freedom, we muſt confider

fome

some operating power as the cause, and some exertion of the power operated upon as an effect to be produced thereby: if such effect will follow as may be expected from the cause, then are we free in the operating power, and our exertion of the operated is our own free act; but if a different effect will follow, then are we under force or restraint.

If we enquire further whether we be free to use this operating power, this is a new question which must be discussed in like manner with the former, by considering the operating power as an effect, and some other power not thought of before as a cause.

For let the mind have ever so much power to act upon herself, either by predetermination, or coexistent election, such her acting is an action as much as acting upon the limbs, and the freedom of it must be tried by the same rules: for as I have freedom of action so long as there lies no bar or obstacle against using my bodily powers in such manner as my Will shall

Free Will.

shall direct, whatever causes may incline me to employ them one particular way; so have I freedom of Will while nothing hinders, but that such volition shall take place as I predetermine or elect, whatever may give occasion to my so determining or electing. For Liberty bears no connection with any thing antecedent [a] to the operation of that power

---

[a] *Chrysippus* and the Stoics, as we find in *Tully de Fato*, placed the freedom of Will in its independance on all external or antecedent causes. Yet they claimed this freedom as the natural privilege of man; and held at the same time, that all his actions, even the minutest of them, were fated. How they reconciled these two opinions, it is difficult to guess.

Their mistake seems to have proceeded from want of distinguishing between efficient, and final causes, the former whereof, being antecedent, destroy free agency, which yet may well consist with the latter. A cannon-ball has no efficacy to beat down a rampart, unless what it receives from the powder, which therefore is an efficient antecedent cause; and consequently, the action of the ball must be necessary. But if you desire your friend to pull down the window-sash, you give no efficacy to his arm, for he does it entirely by his own strength, therefore his action is free: yet your request was the motive, without which he would not have done it; so you are the antecedent, and external cause of what he does.

whose liberty we enquire into, but solely with what shall follow after it, and with the removal of all obstruction which might prevent it from taking effect: therefore may well consist with causes prior to such operation, and with the dominion of that Providence whose disposal those causes lie under.

Thus while we can keep a Disputant to any one settled point, one stated case of acting, or willing, we shall manage well enough with him; but men are apt to dodge about the post, alledging, that we may will as we choose, and choose if we will, without understanding themselves in the use of those terms, or settling the distinction between them; but one moment taking them for synonimous, and the next for different acts producing one another. Whereas if we fix the meaning of choice to a predetermination, then in such cases where our determination stands confined to certain limits, or we are compelled to take a course contrary to that we determine, our volitions, and consequently our

Free Will.

our actions depend upon the causes applying such force or restraint: but in cases where we remain perfectly free to prosecute whatever we may determine upon, they depend upon the motives occurring to our judgement, or imagination in making the determination, or upon our former cares in forming the condition of our mind; which cares depended upon the like causes, and so on as far as the Will was concerned, until you come to some first determination, or act of the mind to which there was no other act preceding [b].

§. 18. As to the coexistent elective power [a], self-moving and independent on all causes, whether

---

[b] Which act must depend upon external causes; and consequently so must all subsequent volitions dependant thereon.

[a] Our Author's zeal against the freewill of indifference urges him to take every occasion of aiming a stroke at it: but his principal attack is carried on in the Chapter of Satisfaction, where in conjunction with Mr. *Locke*, he has pursued it to every corner, and subterfuge under which it might take refuge. But he conceives that the notion of the Will acting without motives,

whether of external objects, motives of judgement and imagination, or prior determinations of our own, if this could once be well established, then farewell to all prudence, deliberation, and dependance upon our own conduct, and that of other people: for what avails it to contrive a plan

motives, took rise from there being many of them latent, unknown even to ourselves; for it is a common remark, that nothing is more deceitful or unfathomable than the heart of man; and from there being many of them so transient that we cannot observe them; besides that the tastes and desires of men being infinitely various, we often find them acting upon inducements, which would not have been such to ourselves, therefore suppose they had none for their proceeding.

Nor need we wonder at his zeal against indifference, because that doctrine once established would overthrow his whole system; which contains an examination of the several species of motives weighing with the mind, the manner of their being generated and introduced to the thought, and the methods of providing ourselves with such as shall be most salutary, and conducive to happiness: in all which he apprehends that Science, reported anciently to have descended from heaven, the knowledge of ourselves, to consist. And his theology depends in great part upon the influence of motives: for he conceives 'tis by their intervention alone, that the government of Providence over the moral world may

plan of my measures ever so wisely, to inculcate salutary maxims upon my mind, to nourish sentiments of honour, or duty, or moral senses for my guidance, if I may afterwards chance to elect the wildest, and most extravagant actions in defiance of all reason, or inclination, or former resolutions to the contrary? or how can I depend that my best and dearest friend will not murder me, while there is a hazard that he may elect in opposition to all the judgement and discretion in his head, the sentiments and desires in his heart?

may be explained; and our expectations in a future life, upon any tolerable grounds, ascertained. For we can discover nothing in all visible nature likely to affect us hereafter, nor can we know any thing of the manner wherein we shall be disposed of otherwise than by so much as we may discover of the character of that Being, who presides over all nature, as well visible as invisible. But the character of an Agent is denominated by the views and motives wherewith he conducts himself. Therefore unless we conceive God likewise to act upon motives, and take final causes under our contemplation, we can gather nothing satisfactory, by the light of reason, concerning our future condition: but the prospect will lie dark, uncertain, and dismal before us.

But

But such terrors as these the most zealous devotees of an elective power do not lie under; they depend upon men's acting conformably to their characters; if they know a hardened villain, they make no question of his electing acts of violence, injury and dishonesty whenever opportunity shall serve, and confide in themselves for making just and wise elections in their future conduct.

What then occasions the difference between man and man? for there must be some cause of the moral character, some account to be given why we know what use each person will make of his elective power. The difference, say they, lies in the Will itself, which has a peculiar bent, or ply, or I know not what, different from that of another person: the villain has a perverseness of Will, therefore will always choose perversely; and they themselves a rectitude of Will, so of course they will choose rightly and wisely. But whence got they this I know not what in their Will? was it innate? was it the natural

constitution

Free Will.

conſtitution of their mind? Then they ought to bleſs the Author of their nature, who gave them this happy conſtitution on creating them. But no, this muſt not be the caſe; for they will loſe all merit of their rectitude, unleſs it was of their own acquiring; therefore they gave this right Ply to their Wills themſelves by their former cares, and induſtry, and right management of their elective power. Be it ſo; for we are in the humour to admit every thing they pleaſe to aſſume; ſtill we muſt aſk, what moved them to ſuch right management? it could not be the Ply of their Will; for if this were acquired, they could not have it before they acquired it, nor could they derive from thence their choice of the right methods taken in the acquiſition. What then, did they light upon thoſe methods by mere chance? I do not ſuſpect they will ſay this; for this would make Virtue nothing more than a lucky hit, which one Simpleton might ſtumble upon as well as another. If then their choice had a ſource, there remains no other

we

we can guefs befides education, example, company, the temperament of their body, ftate of their mental organization [b], objects furrounding them, events touching their notice, and the like; caufes antecedent and external to the mind electing, under the direction of that power whom they muft acknowledge to govern all things external.

§. 19. Upon the whole, we may conclude Freedom, in whatever light we place

[b] A kind of technical term, employed by our Author, to denote a fet of organs compofed of very fine corporeal fubftance, ufed by the mind as her inftrument in meditation, when retired from all external objects. For he conceives the faculty of thinking, or reafoning, not a primary property of the mind, but a refult from her compofition with a certain fyftem of matter; and fuppofes pure created fpirit no more a thinking, than it is a walking, or a fpeaking fubftance. He allows indeed it can always think, whenever united to a proper organization; and fo it can always walk or fpeak, whenever united to a body having legs, or organs of fpeech: but when removed from all matter, it can perform neither function, for want of inftruments to act with, materials and objects to act upon.

Thefe organizations, detached from their grofs bodies, were the vehicles he found inhabiting the vehicular ftate, when tranfported thereinto in the vifion.

it,

it, or to whatever power, whether real or imaginary, apply it, by no means repugnant to the operation of prior caufes moving us to the exercife of that power, nor to the dominion of Providence, having all thofe caufes and their caufes at difpofal. So that the Plan of Providence may well take effect without infringing a tittle upon our Liberty: events which neither our judgement, nor our appetite would incline us to produce, are placed out of our power, and entrufted in the hands of other agents, fo come to pafs by neceffity with refpect to us; the returns of fummer and winter do not depend upon our option, becaufe we might be apt to choofe a perpetual fpring: but wherever God thinks proper to employ us in executing any part of his plan, there needs only to give us the powers, the talents, the opportunities, the judgements, the motives requifite, and we fhall compleat the lines allotted us by the exercife of our freedom.

So far as you can penetrate into a man's fentiments, and defires, and have the proper objects at command, you may put him upon any work you shall require: if money be his idol, and you have enough to bribe him, you may make him do whatever you please; if he make his belly his god, you may draw him from *Millbank* to *Radcliffe-highway* by an exquisite entertainment; or if good nature be his ruling principle, you may employ him in any kind office you shall want. Your politicians know how to turn the passions of men independent on their authority to serve their designs: and the Divine Politician may do this more compleatly, not only as he knows perfectly the secrets of all hearts, but as he gave them that understanding, and those appetites which determine the colour of their actions; and we need not doubt of his having given them such as will effectually answer the purposes intended by them.

In some few instances where we know the hearts of men, we can effect our purposes with them as surely as we can with any corporeal instruments in our hands: if you want to give a ball, or an entertainment,

tainment, 'tis but sending an invitation to persons fond of these diversions, and you will have your company resort to you of their own free choice, nor could you bring them more effectually, if you had the authority of an absolute monarch over them; so that in this instance you govern their motions either to *Hickford's*, or the *Apollo* near *Temple-Bar*, or your own dining-room, without the least impeachment of their liberty. And we have a present example before our eyes of a monarch, who having the love of his subjects, can by their free services resist the combined efforts of the mightiest despotic powers upon earth. Nor can Despotism itself do any great matters without aid of Free Will: for rewards, honours, and encouragements, those engines of free agency, contribute more to the valour of armies, than any scourges of punishment, or peremptory edicts concluding, For such is our Will.

Since then experience testifies, that man can make so much use of liberty towards accomplishing his designs, why should we
scruple

scruple to think the same of God in a larger extent? for he not only has all the objects in his power which touch the springs of action, but fabricated the springs themselves, and set them to receive what touches they shall take.

§. 20. But we judge of the workings of Providence by our own narrow way of proceeding; we take our measures from time to time as the expedience of them occurs to our thoughts, and then must make what use we can of the materials or instruments before us, be they such as exactly suit our purpose, or not; and even if we had the making of our instruments, yet not always knowing what we shall want to do with them, we should often find them inconvenient for our service: nor is it unfrequent that the works we performed yesterday stand in the way of those we are to perform to-day, because new schemes and new occasions of employing ourselves occur to us perpetually [a]. In

---

[a] It is not easy for us to form any conception of the manner of God's working, unless by analogy with our own.

own. Now when we act providently for the future, it is by some operation upon the things about us, to produce effects that would not otherwise have ensued: for when things fall of themselves into the train we desire, there is no room for our activity or prudence to interfere, nor have we any thing more to do, than wait the event. And in this case we may scarce be able to satisfy a by-stander, of their lying under our disposal, unless by making some alteration in their motions, to convince him of our power. In like manner, we look for the manifestation of a Providence, in extraordinary events, and such are commonly produced by those who would enforce the belief of one: as if there were not sufficient evidence in the ordinary courses of nature, while she proceeds in her usual channel of second causes. But we should consider that the case is different between God, and ourselves: there are innumerable causes in act around us, which we did not set at work; nor have our activity and contrivance any other object than what little alterations we can make among them. The woods would grow, and the rivers run, had the earth been never inhabited; but when we see the one cut into regular glades, or the other divided into canals, hollowed along through higher ground, we know the hand of man has been busy among them, and in general, the marks of human industry are found only in such works, as would not have been performed by rude nature. But nature could not have begun any course, unless put into it by the divine appointment; nor could second causes have proceeded to act in any manner, without an energy and direction received from the first. Therefore their operations are an evidence of his power; and their productions, serving the uses of man, an evidence of his Providence, equally convincing with that of extraordinary

traordinary events, to an attentive obferver, taking in the confideration of final caufes; without which, neither evidence would have any avail. For what do we fee in the remarkable changes of wind contributing to bring on the Revolution. The winds vary every day, nor can we gather any thing from the particular variations happening at that time, unlefs we fuppofe God to have had in view the deliverance of thefe kingdoms from Popery and arbitrary power. What fhall we fay to the many caufes concurring at the Reformation? The wilful and imperious temper of the Monarch, fubmiffive difpofition of the people, tired out by long wars between the two rofes, obftinacy of the Roman Pontiff, quarrels between foreign Princes, allowing them no leifure to interfere? How is the hand of Providence difcernible in all this, without the idea of a gracious defign to refcue our forefathers and ourfelves from papal tyranny and fuperftition? And with fome fuch idea we may difcern the fame hand in the powers of nature, whereof we have continual experience. For the fertility of foils, the rife and defcent of vapours, the viciffitudes of feafons, the curious ftructure of veffels and fibres in the tree yielding fruit after his kind, and the herb after his kind, whofe feed is in itfelf, indicate a provident concern and contrivance for the fuftenance of animals, exerted at the creation. The progrefs of arts, manufactures, and fciences; the advancement of knowledge, and thofe accomplifhments rendering nations more civilized, befpeak a kind regard for mankind, and an admirably wife provifion, made at the beginning, enabling them, by the ufe of their natural talents, and the materials prepared to exercife them upon, to rife from the rude and favage fimplicity of ancient times,

to

Free Will.

In like manner we vulgarly imagine [b] God acting occasionally, and taking up purposes to their present better policied, and better accommodated situation. And as these advantages still tend to further improvement, they denote the like regard for the future race of men who shall succeed us while the world endures. Therefore we need not hunt about for strange incidents, and uncommon phenomena, to satisfy us of a providence, which rather wants such testimonies to awaken our attention, than convince our understanding. Even miracles themselves were in ancient language called Signs and Wonders; and the very word by its derivation imports, something exciting our admiration; nor were we to see them worked ourselves, could we esteem them instances of greater power than appear in the stated laws of nature. Neither could we suppose God employing them as necessary means, without which he was not able to have effected his purpose: but rather in condescension to the dulness of our apprehensions, which might have overlooked the purpose, had he compleated it by less striking means. But it would be better for us, if we could so clear our mental eye, as that it might see by the common light; for it argues a defect in the optics, not to discern objects without an extraordinary glare cast upon them. Besides that those who are over fond of these glares, run a great hazard of meeting phantasms and illusions among them.

[b] And this imagination, though represented here in an unfavourable light, does not deserve to be discountenanced, as being the best suited to common capacity. For the plain man can never totally banish the idea of

purposes he had not thought of before until a concurrence of circumstances rendered them expedient: we apprehend him as having turned the numerous race of men loose into the wide world, endowed them with various powers, talents, appetites, and characters, without knowing precisely, or without caring what they will produce: we allow him indeed to have formed the main lines of a plan; but left large vacancies between to be filled up by chance, whose wild workings lie under his controul to divert their course when they would interfere with the strokes of his pencil; for the eye of Providence watches over the motions of human creatures, and when he sees them running counter to his designs, he turns them aside, or guides them by his secret influence to co-operate therewith.

chance out of his system, nor understand the government of Providence, otherwise than by a constant vigilance over the workings of second causes, and occasional interpositions to rectify whatever happens to run amiss: neither does he see wherein this idea derogates in any-wise from the divine Power, or Wisdom, or Omniscience.

Now

Free Will.

Now confidering the vaft variety of humours, the difcordant aims and interefts among mankind, it muft be acknowledged that the government of the world, in this view of it, could not be adminiftered without either continual miraculous interpofitions in the motions of matter, or compulfions and reftraints upon free Agency, giving our volition another turn than it would take from the motives prefent before us, or caufing other motions to arife in our limbs, and thoughts in our minds, than our prefent volition would naturally produce.

But when we reflect that even the wanton gambols of chance muft refult from agents and caufes originally fet at work by the Almighty, when we call to mind his infinite Wifdom and Omnifcience which nothing can efcape, nothing perplex or overload, it feems more congruous with that boundlefs attribute to imagine that no fingle, nor moft diftant effect of the powers and motions he gave was overlooked, no chafms or empty fpaces left in his defign:

but that upon the formation of a world ᵉ he laid a full and perfect plan of all the operations that should ensue during the period of its continuance.

And what interpositions there are (for I would leave every one to his own opinion concerning the frequency, or rarity of them

ᵉ Not creation of the world, as any other person would have expressed it. For our author, though far from a Free-thinker, in the modern sense of the word, that is, a lover of opposition against received tenets, has endeavoured all along to maintain a freedom and openness of thought. But it is dangerous trusting to human reason, which has unluckily led him into a whimsical and unorthodox notion, that this world we inhabit is not the only one God ever created, nor the several species of animals falling within our notice, the only living works of his hands: and that after certain periods, the worlds now subsisting may be dissolved, and new ones fabricated out of the materials. Nay, his fondness for the maxim, Nothing made in vain, will not suffer him to admit any wastes, or vacancies in nature: but he supposes, in his chapter of the Mundane Soul, that all space, not occupied by body, may be replete with spiritual substance, to whom the particles of matter, floating therein, may serve for objects of perception, and subjects of action, and whose ministry may be employed in carrying on the courses of nature according to the laws prescribed for them, or perhaps in forming new worlds upon the plans contrived by infinite Wisdom. Strange! to what wild

lengths

Free Will.

them [d]) how much soever they may operate secretly to us, were not sudden expedients lengths of speculation a lively fancy will sometimes carry people! But my Friend's enthusiasm is excusable, as proceeding from a commendable principle: for he conceives it would give a higher idea of the magnificence of our Creator, to imagine his great kingdom the universe fully peopled, to suppose innumerable hosts of spirits receiving continual supplies of happiness from his inexhaustible bounty, and praising him incessantly by that best of sacrifices, more acceptable than the fat of lambs, an active and willing obedience to his commands, and an unwearied diligence in executing his laws, as well ordinary as extraordinary.

On communicating this note to Mr. *Search*, who is ever sollicitous that none of his vagaries should do hurt to any body, he desired me to caution such of my Readers as may chance to catch the enthusiasm from him, that they give way to it no further than while it may warm their hearts, or raise their ideas, in those seasons only, wherein speculation is proper; but to throw it wholly aside when they enter into the common transactions, and common conversations of life; lest they meet the mishap of that Astronomer who gazing at the stars as he went along, saw nothing of the ground before him, and so plunged headlong into a miry ditch: and above all, to beware of fancying themselves having an intercourse, or being in any discoverable manner affected, with the spiritual substance wherewith he supposes them on all sides closely surrounded.

[d] Mr. *Search*, from the beginning of his enquiries, has proceeded solely upon the fund of natural reason;

not

Free Will.

dients to anfwer unforefeen emergencies, but contained in the original plan, which was purpofely fo framed as to need his interpofing hand when, and where, and as often

not that he means to depreciate the treafures afforded by Revelation, but having not had the reading fufficient for qualifying him to examine the evidences of it, and being defirous of going to the bottom in every part of his work, as being to deal with perfons who will not fuffer him to take any thing upon truft, he thought himfelf intitled to build only upon fuch ground as he found in his poffeffion, to which no man would controvert his right of entry. So he fet out with the examination of human Nature; he then proceeded to contemplate the courfes of things around us, fo far as they fell under our cognizance or obfervation; and from thence to gather what could be difcovered with reafonable affurance, concerning the Author of Nature. He is now returning downwards from the idea of God to the idea of thofe of his works remaining to us invifible: which are not to be counted matters of mere fpeculation, being fuch wherein we ourfelves are likely within a few years to have concern. In this part of his progrefs he is arrived at Providence, the title of his laft preceeding chapter, wherein he entertains fo large an idea of the divine Skill and Omnifcience, as to conceive it poffible, in theory, that God might have compleated his univerfe from everlafting, and refted ever fince from all his works; having formed nature once for all in fuch admirable contrivance, that fhe might run her appointed courfes for ever, without needing any further touch of his hand; the mundane

Free Will.

often as he predetermined to apply it. But in thofe parts wherein he has thought proper to employ us as his inftruments for executing them, to controul us in the exercife

dane foul, or fpiritual fubftance, being provided with activity fufficient to repair the continual decays of motion among matter, occafioned by the collifion of bodies. On the other hand, he did not find it incongruous with his notions of the Deity, to imagine him, in his firft work, purpofely leaving fomething for himself afterwards to do; and laying his fchemes broken in fome parts, that there might be room for further application of his power, at fuch times, and in fuch manner, as he in his wifdom judged proper. So the queftion, Whether interpofition or none, being equally tenable in theory on both fides, remains to be decided by obfervation of facts. But he can find no pofitive evidence (bating thofe recorded in facred Writ, which he cannot take into confideration, as being befide his plan) to fatisfy him of an interpofition, later than the formation of this earth, and the planetary fyftem: fince which, as far as the eye of reafon can difcern, God feems to have refted from his works. Yet he does not defire to hinder others from believing frequent interpofitions, made every day, or every hour of the day, if they fee convincing proofs of them: hoping they will indulge him in retaining his own opinion, until he fhall have fufficient lights afforded him to difcern the truth. And he wifhes every one might be allowed the like liberty, without bringing a difcredit upon himfelf from thofe whom the ufe of it carries a different way. For he thinks men by much too hafty
and

exercise of our powers would be to defeat his own designs, by disturbing the operation of those causes himself had chosen for the accomplishment of them.

Thus and severe upon one another in their censures of Prophaneness and Superstition; the same notions being such to one, which are not so to his neighbour, according to their different apprehensions. The series of causes and events has been compared of old to a golden chain, hanging down from heaven, whereon the earth and elements, with all their contents, whether gods, or men, or animals, or vegetables, are suspended. Now we all agree that this chain is upholden by Almighty Power grasping it at the uppermost link; but which is that uppermost link, we greatly differ, and must necessarily do so while one man can see further, to count more links than another. To make the figure more apposite to our purpose, we will suppose the chain branched out into innumerable smaller ones, sustaining their respective weights among the productions of nature, and issues of fortune. Then in proportion as men have accustomed themselves to look at distant objects, they will acquire a more or less piercing sight; and consequently trace all, or some, or a few only of these little chains to the principal. But wherever they lose the connection, they must place a separate finger at the top of what remains, or the weight will have nothing to support it. Therefore the plain man is not superstitious in conceiving a multitude of interpositions, because without them he cannot conceive how the weight should be upholden by Almighty Power: neither is the studious man prophane in rejecting them,

because

Free Will.

Thus he governs all things in heaven and earth by power and wisdom conjointly, matter by necessity and impulse, brutes by sense and instinct, the blessed spirits above by

becauſe he diſcerns the whole ſuſtained by one effort of that power. For prophaneneſs is the reſting in ſecond cauſes without regard to the firſt; and ſuperſtition the calling in omnipotence needleſly; which muſt neceſſarily vary its form among mankind, as one perſon's needs differ from thoſe of another. But it is recommended to every man to remove the finger of God from him as far as poſſible, provided he never let it go out of ſight: for in ſo doing he will diſcern more of the divine Wiſdom, becauſe there is none in doing every thing by dint of force and authority. Were God to maintain us by raining manna from heaven as we wanted it; this would not diſplay his wiſdom, like the various proviſions he has made for ſupplying us with food by natural means. Were he to ſend his angel every morning to declare what each of us was to do for the day, and ſhower down his irreſiſtible Grace, to carry us through temptations that might urge us to diſobey him wilfully; we ſhould acknowledge his power, and his goodneſs, but ſee nothing of his wiſdom. But when he turns his numerous race of men abroad with various and diſcordant paſſions, inclinations, intereſts, talents, views, and opinions, ſo admirably adjuſted together, and diſtributed among them, as that they fulfil his will, in the accompliſhment of his purpoſes, while they think of nothing leſs: whoever has ſenſe and obſervation enough to underſtand this, muſt adore the wiſe contriver of ſo complicated

by significations of his will, which they gladly and freely set themselves to fulfil, man partly by necessary agents affecting him, partly by laws, restrictions, apprehensions of mischief and danger controuling him, and partly by leaving him to his free choice in following such portion of understanding

a scheme. Now there is a justice to be observed between the attributes, nor must we suffer our zeal for one to magnify it at the expence of another. Therefore let us all, according to the state of our respective imaginations, cast them into such scenes, as may give us the fullest representation of the divine government in all its parts, without disturbing one another in our manner of laying out the prospect. Let not the devout religious man judge hardly of the rationalist, for ascribing all to nature and second causes, because he sees God at the birth of nature, planning down her courses, and giving spring to the causes that produce events of all kinds, as well certain as casual. Neither let the latter deny his less penetrating neighbour the benefit of a perpetual interposition, necessary to him for comprehending the administration of affairs throughout the world; because the powers of nature appear to him as self-moving, and the mazes of fortune struck out every day afresh by the blind ramblings of chance. And I believe if any person of a serious turn will recollect the system of Providence he entertained in his youth, he will find it abounding in interpositions, which as he grew in knowledge and experience have gradually decreased.

standing and appetites as himself has allotted him.

§. 21. Nor need we fancy ourselves always in shackles, because every moment under the dominion and conduct of Providence, for it has been shewn that Liberty has no concern with causes antecedent to the exercise of our power, but solely with what might stand in our way upon such exercise: if I can do what I will, I have freedom of action, no matter how I came to will this or that particular employment: if I can choose as I will, I have freedom of choice, no matter what induced me to make one choice preferably to all others.

What then, are we mere puppets, actuated by springs and wires, because it was given us both to will and to do? By no means; for when they are given us, we have as full and free liberty to use them both, as if they had fallen upon us by chance, or we had made them for ourselves. If my father left me a good portion, I can do the same with it, and have as free disposal

posal of it, as if I had made the gold myself by transmutation with the Philosopher's stone [a]: and if he brought me by the cares of his education, from a lavish temper to prudence

[a] Ned was led into this thought by one of his own foibles: for you must know, he has long since gotten a mighty notion of the Philosopher's stone; only instead of transmuting metals, he wants to transmute error into truth with it. For being of a peaceable disposition, he does not love to overthrow, so much as to transmute. The process whereby he thinks to effect this is, by distinctions, illustrations, constructions, explanations, and other methods known only to Adepts, to pick out the gross particles from some doctrine that has hitherto been found poisonous, and infuse others in their room, thereby giving it a contrary quality. The curious Reader may find him exhibiting a specimen of his art by and by upon prescience, fate, and predestination; which from a lumpish saturnine substance, that used to lie heavy upon the digestion, generating black bile, damping the spirits, benumbing the active powers, and sending up frightful phantoms to the brain, he will attempt to turn into an *aurum potabile*, that shall sit easy upon the stomach, and enliven and invigorate like a salutary cordial. It was his reliance upon this art, that made him keep the former part of his works in reserve: for having picked up some base metals in his researches, he chose not to issue them forth, until he could find means of transmuting them properly into current sterling.

When I have expostulated with him upon the folly of hunting after the Philosopher's stone, he justified

Free Will. 95

prudence and œconomy, this does not impeach my liberty to squander it all away.

Nor have we reason to disturb ourselves with imaginations of a thraldom from secret

himself by the general practice. For, says he, there are multitudes of Trasmutors up and down every where; but the vexation is, they go to work the wrong way, converting gold into base metals. The Papists, Fanatics, and Methodists, have transmuted the golden streams of religion into a kind of Mercury sublimate, that insinuates throughout the constitution, and intoxicates the brain; making men furious or foolish, cursing, damning, and worrying one another to pieces, or giving up their persons, their estates, and their senses to the disposal of their leaders; leaving common sense to run after illuminations, and turning the fancies of men into the counsels of God. The Free-thinkers have transmuted sterling reason into tinsel witticism, productive of self-conceit, and an assurance of victory; for when you begin to joke with a Disputant, you do not deserve to be talked with any longer; so your argument remains unanswerable, and yourself master of the field. Our political writers have trasmuted liberty into licentiousness, and the bare surmise of an infamous peace being intended, into a certain fact, for which a minister ought to be hanged, drawn, and quartered, in the judgement of all the zealous patriots of our tea-tables, coffee-houses, and ale-houses. Since then, says he, these operators have met with such success in the world, it shows there is something in the art: and if they have used it perversely,

cret influences, and unseen springs, when those that are manifest and seen do not work upon us by constraint; for sometimes we may discern the influence that guides us, and yet find no thraldom in following whither it leads.

How much of our employment depends upon the natural appetites of hunger and thirst? You may pretend indeed that these are

versely, why should not I turn it to better service? Nor, if I can produce a single grain of good metal, out of any dross, ought I to incur blame for contributing my mite towards enriching the commonwealth of learning.

Besides, says he, I find the Rosycrucian art very convenient for my private use: for I want no index expurgatorius. I may read *Spinoza*, *Machiavel*, *Tindal*, or *Wesley*'s Journals, with some emolument. For if I cannot do like *Virgil*, who was said to pick up gold out of the dunghill of *Ennius*, yet I may imitate the arch-chymist, Sun, who every day transmutes that filthy substance into roses and lilies, wheat, barley, and wholesome vegetables. Indeed there are some stubborn subjects eluding all the powers of chymistry: such as our weekly Dissertations, popular Declamations, and retailings of Scandal and Obloquy against the Great: for they contain no solid substance at all, and it is impossible to make any thing out of whipped sullabub, or mere colouring.

Free Will.

are acts of neceffity, becaufe we muft eat, or ftarve [b], but follow men to their meals, and you will not fee one in a thoufand that eats becaufe he muft, but becaufe he likes it; which of us ever fits down to table by compulfion, or feels himfelf conftrained to cut the joint before him, or perceives his tongue moved by ftrings like a puppet when he calls for a glafs of wine?

What fhall we fay to the mutual propenfity between the fexes, another main fpring in the hand of God, by which he preferves the race of men upon earth? How many under twigs, what fafhions, contrivances, amufements, accomplifhments, grow from that ftem? but wherein does it check or overfhadow human liberty?

[b] In a former chapter, having occafion to obferve how commonly we miftake our motives of action, he fays, If any body fhould afk, why you take your ftated meals of breakfaft, dinner, and fupper, I warrant you would anfwer, Becaufe I cannot live without eating. But if this were our real motive, we fhould hardly play fo good a knife, or put about the glafs fo brifkly as we do; for we might keep ourfelves alive with a great deal lefs trouble.

Do boys and girls meet together by compulsion, or choice? Is the Miss under a force when she culls among her trinkets with curious toil to tiff herself out in the most engaging manner, or teazes pappa for money to buy a new-fashioned silk? Is the Beau compelled against his Will to practise winning airs before the glass, or employ for whole hours all the thought withinside his noddle to bepowder and becurl the outside[c]?

How strongly does parental instinct operate upon us! 'Tis by this channel that God transmits arts and sciences, education, estates, conveniencies of life, knowledge, and old experience from generation to generation. In this we see the finger of Providence and feel its potent touches[d], yet feel no limitation in our liberty therefrom: for what parent does not willingly go about the provisions he makes for his children,

[c] My friend, like other Philosophers, is a little slovenly in his dress; which makes him the readier to give a sly wipe at the contrary character.

[d] Honest *Ned* speaks experimentally in this place; for nobody is more sensible to these touches than he.

Free Will.

or finds himself under any other direction than his own choice and judgement in the application of his cares for their advantage, or perceives himself moved by clock-work to procure any little toy, or diverfion for them?

§. 22. Our powers of action stand limited to a certain extent of ground, but within the enclofure we may ramble about as we pleafe to take our pafture, or our paftime: fometimes there are reftraints hanging over us, which confine us to particular walks, obligations and duties to be fulfilled, authority to be obeyed, wants to be fupplied, neceffaries of life to be provided, and it behoves us to regard thefe reftrictions, or mifchief will enfue: but in many of our hours we have no limitations upon our conduct, and then we may move eafily and lightly without the weight of any fecret force or impediment encumbering us.

Nor need we fear left we may defeat the purpofes of God, or make any breaches in the plan of his Providence; for he knew what ufes we would make of our Liberty, and has provided his plan accordingly. Let the Princes run madly into broils, and the *Grecians* fuffer, the Will of *Jove* is fulfilled by their madnefs, and will be, whatever conduct man fhall purfue. Therefore we have but our own Will * to take care of; only let us not confult folely

---

* Here underftood, the Will of Inclination. Our Author has fpent a whole chapter in defence of a doctrine that may feem heretical, both in natural and revealed Religion: for his fubject being the *fummum bonum*, or ultimate end of action, he places it folely in every man's own happinefs. But happinefs is the aggregate of pleafures; and pleafures, except fome few of them, which fall upon us unexpectedly from fenfation, confift in the gratification of our refpective defires; for what pleafes one perfon, may give pain to another, who has a contrary tafte. So a man has nothing elfe to do, than ftudy how he may beft gratify his defires. Now this looks like an exhortation to purfue every fudden whim as it ftarts up in our fancy, and will be fo taken, until we fhall fee how he has tranfmuted it. For he fays, this is not the way to gratification: he owns, indeed, that defire is the beft friend we have; becaufe but for it, our lives would pafs infipid and irkfome; neverthelefs he exhorts men not to forget their abfent friends, nor gratify one defire

Free Will.

solely our present Will and Fancy, but pay a due regard to what we may will to-morrow; and in our deliberations and execution of the prudential measures for procuring

desire present to their thoughts, at the expence of another that may sollicit by and by. But when they have divers measures of conduct lying before them for their option, and stand in a situation to discern all the consequences resulting therefrom, let them chuse such as will procure them most gratification upon the whole. If they sit down to a table plentifully stored with high-dressed viands, and find in themselves a strong inclination to eat unmeasurably; while doing this they add to their happiness; therefore so far they do well. But what if such indulgence will bring on sickness of stomach, incapacity for business, conversation, or other diversion, hurt their fortune, or their reputation, or sit heavy upon their conscience: consequences they will vehemently dislike when falling upon them? Or, tho' they do not foresee these effects, yet are warned against them by the moral sense, or rules of sobriety founded upon the general observation of their expedience? If they still indulge, they are very ill providers for gratification. A true lover of money will make any shift rather than call in what he has standing out at interest on good security: and a true lover of pleasure will undergo any self-denial, that tends to greater enjoyment. For 'tis the want of knowing the value of money, that makes the young Spend-thrift encumber his reversions for the sake of raising a sum in hand: and 'tis the like want of knowing the value of happi-

curing what we shall will to have another time, we may proceed with the same freedom as if there were no superiour power [b] over us.

ness, that puts the voluptuous upon mortgaging their future expectations for a little present indulgence.

He observes likewise, that gratification being relative to desire, there are two ways of attaining it: either by procuring the objects of our desire, or by turning desire upon the objects in our power, or which may be convenient for us. If I have port in my cellar, but wish for claret; or if I have claret, but have likewise the gout, to which it would be hurtful; I shall be gratified alike, either by ordering in claret in the one case, and getting rid of my gout in the other; or by bringing myself to a liking of the liquor I have and may drink without inconvenience. Now men are ready enough of their own accord to pursue the former of these two methods: so the Moralist need only exhort them to the latter. And it becomes the Miser in happiness to take that of the two upon every occasion which he finds the most feasible, or likely to yield him the greatest income. If he has money enough to spare for the claret, or a sure specific against the gout, he will please his palate: but if he knows not where to get either of these, he will enure his mind to enjoy herself over a glass of common port.

[b] He does not mean, no authority it is incumbent upon us to regard, but no stronger power able to controul us in the exercise of our faculties.

Free Will.

And the moſt uſeful deliberation we can enter upon, is how to enlarge our freedom, for all are ready enough to allow that Happineſs conſiſts in liberty to do what we will, nor ſhall I contradict them, ſo they do not reſtrain Will to that of the preſent moment. We commonly underſtand by our Will what our Judgement repreſents as moſt eligible, or our Inclination prompts to as moſt alluring; and whenever theſe two coincide, our Will is quite free; therefore ſo far as we can bring deſire to tally with reaſon, we ſhall enlarge the bounds of our liberty; and if we could do this compleatly ſo as to make a virtue of every neceſſity, and a pleaſure of every obligation, we ſhould never have any reſtraint hanging over us, but attain a perfect liberty; becauſe willing always what was right and feaſible, we ſhould always do what we would.

And this perfect liberty would more apparently, though not more really coincide with the plan of Providence than that pittance of it we now poſſeſs; for then we ſhould

should fulfill the Will of God knowingly, whereas now we fulfill it, but unknowingly, and many times by setting ourselves most strenuously to oppose it.

Foreknowledge. §. 23. And now we might think the controversy ended, and all difficulties got over, the freedom of Will being fully reconciled with the authority and dominion of God: but the busy mind of man, ingenious in finding new perplexities to involve itself in, will not let us rest quiet so; but seeing light open upon one spot, shifts the scene to some other corner, where it may cover itself with clouds and obscurity; and as if fond of slavery, endeavours to derive a title thereto from another quarter, namely, that of Foreknowledge.

For, say the fine Reasoners, if your actions are foreknown, you can do no otherwise than it is known you will do; so your hands are tied down to one particular manner of proceeding, nor are you at liberty to take any other than that you shall pursue.

But

Foreknowledge.

But why so? what connection is there between another's knowledge, and my behaviour? it may possibly direct his own measures, but has no influence at all upon mine. You allow that while my actions remain unknown to every body I may be free; what then if after my being in possession of this freedom some shrewd Politician should discover what I will do, how does that divest me of it, in what respect alter my condition, or by what channel of communication does his discovery operate upon me?

No, say they, you mistake the grounds of our objection; we do not assign his knowledge as a cause of any thing you do, nor pretend it lays any restraint upon your liberty; we only produce it as an evidence of another restraint hanging over you; for he could not know how you will behave, unless it were certain; therefore his knowing is a proof that you will certainly do as he knows; but what will certainly come to pass cannot fall out otherwise; so you have no liberty left, because you cannot do what will never be done.

But how does this alter the case? wherein is the difference between Certainty and Knowledge? Why yes, the difference lies here, that Certainty is the object of Knowledge, though she may not have cast her eye upon it; therefore is a different thing, as having existed before it; for your discovery did not make the Certainty, but presupposes it; for the thing was certain before, though you did not know it.

But what sort of thing is this Certainty to which you ascribe such irresistible force? let us know what rank of Beings to place it under? is it a substance? or if a quality or accident, in what substance does it reside? for we generally apply it to propositions which are only judgements of the mind. It is no agent, it is no power, nor has any efficacy in its state of pre-existence to knowledge; for were it ever so certain the house was on fire, this would influence none of my actions until I know it.

§. 24.

Foreknowledge.

§. 24. If Certainties have any active virtue, it is to generate one another; all our rules of logic fhow us that fome truths are fuch in confequence of other truths: if it certainly will rain to-morrow, it is certain there will be clouds in the air; if it be certain the gun I make tryal of will go off, then the flint will certainly ftrike fire; and in general the certainty of Events infers the certainty of all caufes operating to produce them: therefore whatever acts of my Freewill are certain, I muft certainly have the freedom to do them.

We may indeed frame propofitions concerning future events, without thinking of the manner how they will come to pafs; but remember your own obfervation, that knowledge does not make certainty, but finds it; much lefs can any form of words make, or the omiffion of them deftroy it: therefore whether you fpeak and think of them or no, the fame propofitions may be applied, and the fame certainty belong to the operating caufes, be they Force or

Free-

Freewill, as to the events, and the certainty of each reciprocally, implies the other.

Suppose you under an engagement to meet a person at any particular place, and have a strong inclination to go somewhere else, nevertheless you have too much honour to break your word; but perhaps the man will send five minutes hence to release you from the engagement, and then you will go where you like: now if it be certain you shall go there, must it not be equally certain the restraint will be taken off, and you set at perfect liberty to follow your choice? And if any body had affirmed both a thousand years ago, he would have spoken truth; for while the one remained fortuitous, the other could not be certain: so likewise in all instances of free Agency, the certainty of the action casts a certainty upon the freedom of the Agent; and the certain Foreknowledge of our voluntary proceedings is so far from overthrowing, that it establishes human liberty upon a firmer bottom than it has really belonging to it.

For

Foreknowledge.

For we may obferve further, that this argument unluckily proves too much; becaufe if whatever fhall happen, it be abfolutely impoffible that it fhould not happen; then in fuch inftances wherein we have our freedom, the debarring us the ufe of it was from all eternity an abfolute impoffibility, infurmountable even by Omnipotence itfelf; fo that inftead of being dependant in all our motions upon neceffary caufes, we fhall become independent on the firft, the fupreme Fountain of all power and action.

And for ought I know, the Devil might have employed this fophifm when he rebelled, to prove himfelf his own mafter; for feeling himfelf in poffeffion of freedom, it was always true, that he fhould be free; nor could Omnipotence itfelf prevent his being fo: or he might have beguiled himfelf into his fall, and juftified his difobedience, by arguing in the following manner. If any one had faid before I was made, that I fhould be, he would have fpoken truth; therefore it was certain that

I should be, therefore an absolute impossibility that I should not be; so God could not help creating me, nor do I owe any thanks to the Almighty for my existence.

§. 25. What dependance or countenance does this argument deserve? which is such a *Drawcansir* as to cut down both friend and foe; or like a swivel gun, may be pointed upon any quarter, fore and aft, starboard and larboard; and what is worse, we find it generally, in the hands of sloth and depravity, turned against the lawful authority of reason and prudence.

For when men are too lazy to bestir themselves, or too fond of a foolish thing to be put aside from it by their clearest judgement, they then catch hold of this idle pretence, what will be, must be; therefore why need I take pains, or deliberate at all? for my actions will have some certain issue, and if certain, it is necessary, and if necessary, the event will work itself out some how or other, without my giving myself any trouble to compass it.

But

Foreknowledge.

But who ever argues in this manner, when they have some favourite passion to gratify? They then can study and contrive, set all their wits to work, and use all their might to accomplish their designs: whereas if they think consistently, there is the same certainty in matters of inclination, as of prudence and duty; whatever they wish, must have some certain issue one way or other, and is either unattainable in spite of their utmost endeavours, or will drop into their mouths without their seeking. And thus they may go on to argue themselves out of all activity whatever, so as neither to take up the victuals from their plate, or move away from the fire when it burns their shins.

§. 26. But these fantastical remoras do not obstruct us in the familiar transactions of life, nor do they ever enter into the head of a common man. If a poor fellow has done me some signal service, and I call to him — Hark ye, *Tim*; do you see that sack of pease in the barn-floor yonder?
there

there are a couple of guineas in it somewhere; if you can find them they are your own. Now I know well enough he will get the money; for he will take out every pea one by one but he will come at it; but I know as well that he cannot find it without a good deal of pains and rummaging.

Suppose one of your profound Speculatists were by, and should tell him, Why, *Tim*, you need not put yourself in a hurry to go a rummaging; you may as well sit with your nose over the kitchen fire; for *Search* knows you will get the money; therefore it is a thing certain, and you must have it whether you do any thing, or no. This logic would hardly prevail upon *Tim* to stop his speed for a moment.

Or suppose another subtile refiner sets the matter in a different light: *Tim*, says he, is a mere machine in this case utterly destitute of liberty; for not only his getting the money, but his rummaging the sack is foreknown; so his action is certain and necessary, nor can he help rummaging any more than the great clock can help striking.

Tim

Foreknowledge.

Tim being an arch fellow replies, Ay, but Mafter, for all that I could ftay here and never meddle with the fack, if I were fool enough to run the hazard of fomebody elfe getting away the money before me; and if you'll give me three and forty fhillings to try, I'll fhow you what I can do.

How many times a day do we foreknow our own actions, and thofe of other people, yet feel ourfelves and perceive them free in the performance? Our liberty is fo apparent that the Philofopher with his microfcope [a], and the Ploughman with his half an eye, can difcern it diftinctly through the veil of Certainty and Foreknowledge: 'tis only the half-reafoner, who hangs between both,

[a] Our Author difcovered his having a Microfcope while at work on his chapter of Satisfaction, on happening for once to fpin a thread fomewhat finer than Mr. *Locke*. He feemed mightily pleafed with it, as finding it affift him greatly in his tranfmutations; and talked much of it at firft, but has not mentioned it a good while until now. Yet he ftill continues to ufe it, as the difcerning Reader may perceive, by fome microfcopic obfervations upon Liberty, upon Agency, Volency,

Foreknowledge.

both, and ufes a glafs full of flaws, that hunts for it in vain, or fees it confufedly.

§. 27. It is the crinkles in this glafs making objects appear double, and reprefenting each individual as two diftinct things, which produces that diftinction urged by fome people between human Prefcience and divine, as if one might be compatible with human Liberty, though the other were repugnant.

But why fo? for it is not the party knowing, but the intrinfic certainty of the fact that lays the reftraint: now as man cannot know what is uncertain, fo neither if there were any thing abfolutely fortuitous,

---

Volency, and Electancy; upon Powers operating, or operated upon, in §. 2, 13, 17, & *paffim.* He fays, this little inftrument is abfolutely neceffary for a Mathematician or a Philofopher; but a common magnifying glafs, fuch as we buy for children to play with, will do well enough for a Freethinker; becaufe it ferves to difcover doubts and objections, that a man with his common fenfes would never think of, and magnifies them fufficiently, but fcarce ever reaches to a folution.

could

Foreknowledge.
could it be foreknown even to God [a]; therefore Knowledge, wherever residing, is alike evidence of Certainty.

Very true, say they, where the knowledge is of the same kind; but our's is only conjectural; whereas that of God is absolute: we all confess the human Understanding fallible at best, nor ever so sure of her hits, but there remains a possibility of her being mistaken, and it is this possibility that opens the door to Liberty.

Here, by the way, I cannot help remarking how ready some folks are to blow hot and cold with the same breath, as either serves the turn: if I happen in company to drop a hint like those suggested in my chapter on Judgement [b], that Certainty, mathematical

[a] There are some who hold Eternity a standing point with him, and the future to be equally present with the current moment: but in this case the Knowledge would not be Prescience, but direct Intuition, which does not affect the Argument before us.

[b] Where the Author falls into downright Scepticism: for after having overthrown all Knowledge, except of one thing, which is that we know nothng, he proceeds to take away this too, and proves demonstratively, that

mathematical Certainty, was not made for man, and that we know no more, if so much, than the appearances exhibited this present moment to our senses, and the ideas actually in our thought; I am exclaimed against for an arrant Sceptic, a Visionary, a Trifler, advancing things I do not believe myself. What! cry they, do not we know certainly that the Judges will sit in *Westminster-hall* this term; that the Servant will lay the cloth for dinner; that we ourselves shall go to bed to-night? Yet these very people, like crafty Politicians, now the interests of their argument require it, can take the opposite side, and strike up a coalition with the fallibility of human

that we dont know whether we know any thing or not. For which *Socrates* in the vision compliments him, as being a wiser man than himself, who was declared wisest by the Oracle: for he it seems had fancied he did know that he knew nothing; whereas our Author's greater sagacity had discovered that he did not know even this.

I need not tell the Reader, he made his escape out of this dungeon, because he finds him abroad in open daylight, pretending to know several things in the very last Section.

Under-

Foreknowledge.

Understanding in her strongest assurances. Perhaps the Judges will not sit, for the hall may be swallowed up by an earthquake; perhaps the Servant will not lay the cloth, for he may be struck with an apoplexy; perhaps we shall not go to bed, for the house may take fire: Were these casualties, which depend upon external causes, alledged in diminution of Liberty, they might carry some weight; but what efficacy they can have to encrease it, I cannot discern with best use of the microscope.

But waving this, if bare Possibility may give opening enough to set us free, this same Mr. *Liberty* must be a very slender gentleman, to creep in at such an auger-hole: yet let us consider whether he does get his whole body through, or only thrust in a little finger at most; for we have seen there are degrees of Liberty consistent with a partial Restraint. When I put on my great coat and boots, I can still move my limbs, though not so freely as before: when in town I have not the same liberty as in the

the country; I must not go out in my cap and slippers; I must not carry a bundle under my arm; if *Elizabetha Petrowna*, whom I never saw nor cared for, happens to die two thousand miles off, I must not wear a coloured coat, for so the great goddess, *Fashion*, that *Diana* of *Ephesus*, whom all the world worshippeth, ordains; yet she graciously allows me some latitude in my dress and motions; for I may go armed with a sword I know not how to use, and saunter away the day in coffeehouses, or spend the night in tossing about a pack of cards, without offence to her delicacy.

Now I believe my Antagonists and I, how slightingly soever we have spoken of human Understanding, shall agree that in some instances our Knowledge grounds upon evidence, which makes it a million to one we are in the right: and since an Event may be probable, as well as certain, though we do not know so much, it must then contain an intrinsic probability independent on our knowledge or conjecture.

But

Foreknowledge.

But this probability, being so near of kin to certainty, that the acutest Philosophers could never find a criterion to distinguish them, may be presumed to have the family strength, though not in equal measure; and if one totally overthrows liberty, the other must fasten a clog upon it proportionable to the degree of the probability; so that in cases of the highest assurance we should find ourselves reduced to the condition of a person who should have so many weights hung about him, that one millionth part added more, would render him uncapable of stirring at all.

§. 28. But if this will not do, and they insist upon Probability being totally different from Certainty in kind and efficacy, and that one has no force at all, though the other be irresistible, let them contemplate an object, wherein they must needs acknowledge both perpetual Freedom and absolute Foreknowledge; for I hope they will not deny God to be perfectly free in all his proceedings. If there be such a thing in nature as freedom, where can it reside, if not in the supreme Author of all powers, to whom there is nothing superior that might controul him? Yet I suppose they will scarce imagine all his measures sudden, and his actions fortuitous, or that he does not know to-day what he will do to-morrow.

But if certainty infers necessity, then either he foresees no better than we do, that is conjecturally, when he will stop the torrents of blood that overwhelm *Europe*, the distresses, the ruins, the havock and desolation that spread over land and sea, and restore peace to Christendom, or his hands in the interim remain tied to do it at one precise time, nor is he at liberty to advance the happy event one moment sooner[a]. Nay, we shall not stop here; for if a proposition had been affirmed from everlasting concerning any work of Providence that has been performed, it would have been true: therefore God from all

---

[a] This was wrote before any overtures for a treaty of Pacification were publickly known.

eternity

Foreknowledge.

eternity was necessitated to create and govern his worlds precisely in the manner he has done; and so, according to the devilish fine reasoning used at the end of §. 24. we are not obliged to him, but to the iron-handed goddess Necessity, for our life, our health, our daily bread, and all the blessings we receive.

Perhaps they will alledge the case is different here; for the acts of God are such only as he had determined upon himself, therefore in performing them he executed his own will: but let them remember, that they placed the necessity in the intrinsic certainty of the fact, not in the causes operating to produce it; for if they admit these, then the cause of our free actions being the freedom we have to perform them, will evidence itself, instead of proving our bondage: but, according to them, when a fact is certain, it is necessary, no matter why, or how, it came to be so; and equally certain, whether proceeding from the agent's own determination or some external cause: for if what will be, must be, then whatever

God

God foreknows will be done by himself as well as by us, becomes alike certain, nor can even omnipotence prevent it from taking effect [b].

Thus we see the same ill luck attends the argument wherever we turn it; for if it proves any thing, it proves more than it should; nor can it infringe upon human liberty, without encroaching upon God himself.

Neither let them throw in my teeth what I have reported from *Pythagoras* concerning the oath of *Jove*; for this was only a figurative expression, to denote the unchangeableness of the divine nature: if God has sworn, his oath is sacred, because we know

---

[b] To this argument might be added another. For I suppose every pious man esteems it certain, that God will reward the good and punish the evil-doer; that he will maintain the laws of nature, not throw all things into confusion, nor annihilate the beings he has created. Thus human prescience extends in some cases to the divine agency. But if certainty inferred necessity, then either God must not be free to dispose of us in what manner he judges proper, or it must remain totally uncertain how he will use his power.

he

Foreknowledge. 123

he will keep it [c], being not liable, like man, to change his fentiments, or defign one thing to-day and the contrary to-morrow; but nobody imagines him under any compulfion or neceffity, in cafe he could be fuppofed at any time defirous of violating it; fo that when he performs, he acts with the

[c] Being part of the lecture delivered in the vifion. From which oath the laws of nature received their ftability, and the courfes of events befalling men their certain appointment. *Dacier* would have faid, the philofopher took this hint from the covenant made with *Noah*, that day and night, feed-time and harveft, fhould never fail. And our Rofycrucian took the hint from *Dacier*, to practife with his art chymical upon the fublime myfteries imparted to him. For the Samian fage having broached fo many heathenifh inventions of a preexiftence, a mundane foul, difcerptions and abforptions, tranfmigrations, eternity *à parte ante* of created beings, limited duration of punifhments, homogenity of fpirits, their differences refulting from their refpective compofitions with matter, that he was afraid of being thought a bad man himfelf for conforting with fuch wicked company. So he went to work upon his tranfmuting procefs, wherein he fucceeded fo luckily, that having ventured to read over the whole lecture to a learned divine, a man of a very good difcernment, he cried out at the conclufion, with a kind of rapturous furprize: Why *Search!* you have made *Pythagoras* an orthodox Chriftian.

fame

same pure bounty and unlimited freedom as when he promises.

§. 29. When we examine what gave rise to this notable discovery of every thing certain being necessary, we shall find it spring from a mere quibble of words. What you will do, say they, you must do; for you cannot do otherwise so long as you are to do that, because you cannot do both. Who doubts it? Therefore I allow this to be matter of necessity, not of prudence; nor would I recommend it to any man to deliberate, or make trial, how he shall run and sit still at the same time, or ride on horseback while he goes in a coach: but for all that, what ails him that he might not omit the thing he has resolved upon, or will do, and take a contrary course? How sure soever I am of going to bed, still I may sit up all night, if I please, for neither God nor man hinders me; but I know I shall not, because I know it is in my option, and know what I chuse to do: so my knowledge stands upon my freedom; for if I had it not, I might be compelled to do

what

Foreknowledge.

what I do not chuse, and my action would be uncertain.

But my Knowledge they say is only conjectural. What then? does not God know it too? and does not he know likewise, that he has left the issue to my option? and whether he has given me so much discretion as will withhold me from doing a silly thing merely to shew what I can do? So these three points of Knowledge, the Discretion, the Liberty to use it, and the Event, are so far from overthrowing that they sustain and strengthen one another.

The difficulties we make spring from our conceiving too narrowly of the divine prescience; we consider God as foreknowing an event separately, without knowing, or without contemplating the causes giving it birth: in this case indeed the Foreknowledge must have a something, an inexplicable fatality attending it, for else it could not be absolute, because there might some unforeseen cause intervene to render it abortive. But the prescience of God is universal as well as absolute; when he knows what

will

will come to pass, he knows the causes himself has provided for accomplishing it, nor can any body who considers the matter at all imagine him ever ignorant or forgetful of either; nay, he knows the one, because he knows the other: for if we could suppose him ignorant of the causes, he would not know their issue: therefore in such instances where freedom is one of those causes, he foreknows that freedom, the motives inclining us to use it, and how those motives will operate; and consequently by the rule insisted on, it is as necessary we should enjoy that freedom, as in what manner we shall employ it.

§. 30. Nevertheless they go on still to urge, that we cannot do otherwise than we shall do, not only because we cannot do both, but because we cannot omit what we certainly shall do, and take another course: for an event that will certainly happen, cannot fail of coming to pass, nor can the contrary take effect; but the divine prescience is an irrefragable evidence of this

cer

Foreknowledge.

certainty, becaufe if the thing were uncertain, the Foreknowledge could not be abfolute. Now there is no poffibility that God fhould be miftaken; therefore none that any thing foreknown by him fhould not take effect, or the contrary fhould fall out; then it is not poffible for us to omit whatever it is impoffible fhould fail of being done; fo our power is gone; or if we have a natural ability either to do or to omit, we have no liberty to ufe it, being confined to that particular way which is foreknown.

Now if they will pleafe to throw this curious reafoning into the logical form of a fyllogifm, we may chance to fhew them it has four terms, and therefore concludes nothing. Whatever God foreknows, it is impoffible the contrary fhould be done; what is impoffible to be done, it is out of my power to do; therefore whatever God foreknows, it is out of my power to do the contrary.

I fhall not deny *major* nor *minor*; but if the word *impoffible* fhould carry different fenfes as it ftands in either, the whole chain will become a rope of fand, and the confequence sequence limp lame behind.—In order to canvass this point, let us have recourse to our present patroness, Philology, to mark out the several uses wherein we employ that term, together with others relative thereto, such as, *must*, *may*, *can*, *necessary*, and the like, both in our familiar and serious discourses.

Possible, relates originally and most obviously to Power; for things are possible as far as we have power to perform them, but no farther: and if it be asked, Whether it is possible to transmute lead into gold? you will understand by the question, whether it is in the power of man, by chymical process, or any other art or contrivance, to effect it.

But we often apply the term where we have nothing of power in our thoughts. Suppose, in playing at whist, I have only two cards left in my hand, but must win both tricks to save the game; my partner leads a trump, and the king was turned up on my left hand, in this case I shall put down the ace with hopes of succeeding, because

it

Foreknowledge.

it is poffible the king may be alone. Now by poffible, I do not mean in the power of any body, or any thing, to make the king alone, or guarded: if chance ever had any power, fhe has executed it as foon as the cards were fhuffled and cut, nor has fhe now any further concern in the affair. Therefore here the term denotes only the contingency of what other card lies in the fame hand with the king, and is relative; for to him who holds the cards it is not poffible they fhould be any other than what he fees them, though to me who do not fee them, guarded or not guarded are equally poffible.

On the other hand, whoever confiders the pains I have taken on this crabbed fubject, will think it impoffible I fhould throw my labours into the fire as foon as I have compleated them: not that he thinks any thing of my powers, or fuppofes me to plod on until my arm is fo benumbed that I cannot extend it to the grate, or that I write upon cloth of Afbeftos, which will not confume in the Flames, but becaufe he

thinks

Foreknowledge.

thinks there is no chance I should instantly destroy what I have been so earnest to produce.

Thus Possible sometimes denotes the Power or Liberty we have to do a thing, as Impossible does the want of it, and sometimes only the contingency, or our knowledge or ignorance of an event, without the least reference to the powers producing it. There may be different degrees of possibility in what manner I shall spend my afternoon, according as people know more or less of my character, disposition, or ways of employing my time: but my power and my liberty must be the same, whatever other folks think of me, or though there should be a hundred different opinions or degrees of knowledge about me. If I am under engagement to go with another whither he wants me, and somebody asks which way I am bound, I may say, 'tis possible to the Exchange, or 'tis possible to St. James's, but this leaves me no more at liberty than if it were absolutely impossible that one of them should not be the place. Or if I want

Foreknowledge.

speak with a person whom I know not readily where he is, but am so sure of finding him, that I say it is impossible but I must see him; this does not abridge or any ways alter the liberty I should have to pursue or forbear my enquiries, were it possible my endeavours might prove ineffectual.

It avails nothing to tell us, that our knowledge at best can amount only to the highest probability of conjecture; for our business now lies with the propriety of language, and natural import of those expressions, wherein we use the words Possible or Impossible: whatever refined notions we may have in our closets, we leave them behind, and take up common conceptions when we go abroad upon our common transactions; be our clearest knowledge ever so conjectural, we esteem it certain upon these occasions: which of us in setting out upon a visit, a diversion, or an affair of business, apprehends a possibility of not arriving at the place of his destination, yet at the same time does not apprehend himself at liberty to alter his course in any part of his progress? but if the impossibility of an event failing, implied necessity in the agent, the idea of such impossibility, however erroneous, yet while entertained, must banish the idea of freedom; but whether it does so, I appeal to the judgement and hourly experience of all mankind. And if our Antagonists have found a new sense in the word Impossible, unknown to the rest of the world, they will do well to explain their idea in a manner enabling us to understand their peculiar meaning.

To consider the other words of the like import, we say it may rain, or be fair to-morrow; and when we say this, we think nothing of any choice in the clouds, or the air to produce either weather, as the word naturally implies; for what we may do lies in our option to do, or to forbear. And it is one thing, when speaking of a prisoner for debt, for whom we have just procured a release, we say, Now he may go home to his family; and quite another, when speaking of a person gone out upon

a tour

Foreknowledge.

a tour of diverfion, we fay, He may come home to-day: in one cafe, May expreffes the liberty he has to do as he likes; in the other, it denotes only the chance there is in what manner he will ufe his liberty; for though I fhould know the releafed debtor will not go home, ftill I fhall think he may if he will; but if I know the traveller's intention to ftay out longer, I fhall not think it poffible he may come home to-day.

Nor fhould we fcruple to ufe the word Can upon this occafion; for if we judge it not poffible that he may come, it is the fame thing as believing it certain he cannot come, yet without idea of any imbecillity or reftraint to prevent him.

So likewife Muft and Neceffary, confidered by themfelves, imply a force compelling to one particular action, or an unfurmountable bar againft all others: if I muft attend upon a tryal, I am not at liberty to ftay away; if my health renders exercife neceffary, I muft go abroad fome how or other, and in that cafe am neceffitated to walk when debarred the use of all conveyances. But suppose a friend has some business with me, which requires no sort of haste, but I know he loves to take the first convenient opportunity for dispatching whatever he has to do: upon being asked when I expect to see him, I may say, perhaps not to-day, nor to-morrow, nor all this week; but I think he must necessarily come before the month is out.

Nor do we scruple applying the same terms to things inanimate, which though really necessary agents, we generally conceive and speak of as having powers and liberty. Water compressed in a fire engine must necessarily rush through the spout, being forced to mount upwards against its nature, and because it can find no other vent. But if a careless servant does not mind to thrust the spigot fast into the barrel, the beer must necessarily run all away: in using this expression, we think nothing of the force of gravitation impelling bodies downwards, but only the certainty of the mischief ensuing which we apprehend, for that the liquor

Foreknowledge.

liquor being left to its liberty will follow the natural propenfity it has to defcend, and will exert a power to drive away the loofe fpigot obftructing its paffage.

§. 31. Any body with a little attention, may recollect a thoufand inftances wherein the impoffibility of an event not coming to pafs, implies no more than a denial of all hazard that it may not come to pafs, which is neither an affirmation nor denial of power or freedom in the caufes bringing it forth to produce the contrary. Therefore in cafes where we need not, or lie under no neceffity of doing a thing, where we can, and may, and it is eafily poffible for us to act differently, yet we may be fo fure of our meafures as that they muft neceffarily take effect, that they cannot, there is an impoffibility they fhould fail of fucceeding, or we fhould omit to employ them; which latter impoffibility is a foundation ftrong enough to fupport the higheft degree of Foreknowledge, and confequently Foreknowledge may well be abfolute without putting

putting a force upon us, or cramping us the least in our liberty.

Thus have I endeavoured to rescue mankind from slavery, from the dread of force, restraint and controul hanging continually over them, not like *Epicurus* by pulling Providence from her throne, and setting up the Anarchy of Chance in her stead; but by showing the consistency of her government with the free use of those powers allotted us, and proving human liberty one of the ministers to execute her purposes.

If the foregoing Observations upon this dark and intricate Subject shall render it intelligible to others, and shall have the same weight upom them as they seem to me to deserve; then in those seasons wherein, as I may say, God gives them a holiday to follow their own inclinations, they will move briskly and cheerfully, without thought of any other restraint than, what I hope they will never wish to throw aside, Innocence and Propriety; and when he calls them to his services, if they do but manage to bring their minds into a proper

dispo-

disposition, they will find the performance of them a state of perfect Freedom.

§. 32. Nevertheless we have not done with our Disputants yet, for if we can defend our Liberty against infringement by universal Providence and absolute Foreknowledge, they change their attack upon another quarter, namely, the justice of Reward and Punishment in the situation of mankind we have represented: for, say they, if the Will of God be fulfilled on earth as well as in heaven, who hath ever resisted his Will? why then doth he punish? As to Reward, they find no fault with that being conferred upon them unmerited, so the only difficulty remains with respect to punishment; and in order to answer their question, let us examine what is the proper and natural foundation of Punishment.

Men are apt enough to inflict it for injuries received, with no other view than to wreak their resentment, and the Righteous, when having most compleatly mastered
their

their paſſions, ſtill feel an abhorrence riſe in their breaſts againſt enormous crimes, although no ways affecting themſelves, nor capable of hurting them. What then, is this Reſentment and this Abhorrence innate? Suppoſe they were, yet we cannot aſcribe our paſſions and averſions to the Almighty, or imagine him puniſhing in order to remove a loathſome object from his ſight which it gives him pain to behold. But Mr. *Locke* has long ſince exploded the doctrine of innate Ideas, and if the idea of Injury was acquired, thoſe of Reſentment and Abhorrence, being its offspring, muſt be younger.

In our chapter on the Paſſions we have traced Anger[a] to its origin, and found it derived from Expedience; for children having often relieved themſelves from whatever

---

[a] He ſays, we paſs through four ſtages at leaſt in our progreſs to the paſſion of anger: the experience of damage brought upon us by others; of our power to give them diſpleaſure; of the effect of ſuch diſpleaſure to make them alter their meaſures, and of the oppoſition we muſt expect to meet with againſt the exertion of

Demerit.

ever oppreffed them by a violent exertion of their power againſt the caufe of it, contract a habit of violence, and practife it afterwards without view to the confequences, fatisfaction being tranſlated [b] from the end to the means.

The

of this power. Which laſt gives anger its violence, becaufe a ſtrenuous exertion is neceſſary to furmount that oppofition. But after having compleated our progreſs, we lofe fight of the ſtages leading to it, and then the defire of revenge rifes habitually upon fight of injury, without any further thought.

[b] There is a chapter upon Tranſlation; which is the principal channel whereby our motives are derived from one another. For the fatisfaction apprehended in attaining a purpofe, is what makes it a motive of action with us. Now when there are means neceſſary to be purfued in order to accomplifh this point, our defire of the end caſts a fatisfaction likewife upon the means: fo long as we retain the end in view, that is properly our motive, and we defire the means only for the fake of what they will conduct us to: but it very frequently happens, that the fame means bring us fo often to our defired end, that the fatisfaction thrown from it, reſts at laſt upon them, and we continue our fondneſs for them after the end is dropped out of our thought. Then it is the tranſlation is perfectly made; and the means become an end, or motive, capable of influencing us to action.

This matter is illuſtrated by the inſtance of money, which every body allows would have no regard, unleſs

for

Demerit.

The abhorrence of villainy, as well when proposed to ourselves, as practised by others, is one of the moral senses ^c, which we have shown in the proper place, issue from the same fountain: they may indeed be conveyed to particular persons by education, by precept, by example, and sympathy,

for sake of the conveniences and pleasures of life it procures us. Yet we find it so constantly tending to this end, that there are few of us who would not take some pains, and feel satisfaction in getting a sum, without thinking of the pretty things we could do with it: and in some the satisfaction is so strongly translated, that they will deny themselves those very conveniences which rendered it desirable, for the sake of saving their money.

And as satisfaction is translated from end to means, so is assent, or judgement, from the premises to the conclusion resulting therefrom, which being once well settled in the mind, we continue to look upon as a certain truth, after having utterly forgotten the evidence by which we were brought to acknowledge it for such.

Thus it is by translation we receive all our stores of knowledge, except what is thrown in immediately from the senses: and by the same channel we derive all our motives and desires, except those excited by sensation.

^c Mr. *Search* will not allow them to be given immediately by nature, but either catched by sympathy from others, or formed by translation; which latter is of two sorts,

forts, as we have seen in the preceeding note. For education, precept, and example, operate by information of the judgement concerning the rectitude of the things taught, or seen practised; but sometimes he supposes them acquired by satisfaction translated from those desirable ends to which they have been observed to conduce. And he thinks his opinion confirmed by the great difference of moral senses among mankind: one man places his point of honour in revenging an affront; another in making his payments punctually, another in suffering no waste of his time, another in having nothing to do: one esteems persecution meritorious; another looks upon it with horror and detestation; nor perhaps are there any two men, who see the same things, with equal degree of approbation or abhorrence. But if these senses were natural, not acquired, why should they not represent their objects in the same colours to every body? For all men see whiteness in lilies, redness in roses, and verdure in the grass. Nor let it be said that bad company, or vicious courses, may debilitate or corrupt the senses nature gave us; for the company a man keeps, or vices he practises, will not make him blind or deaf, nor see different colours, or hear different sounds from other people. Or if intemperance does sometimes weaken and vitiate the bodily senses, it does so with respect to all objects alike: a jaundiced eye sees every thing yellow, nor does it add a particular brightness to some colours above the rest: but the moral sense often discerns the lustre of some virtues remarkably well, and sees none at all, or perhaps a darkness in others equally resplendent. Neither is it an objection that some objects appear generally amiable or detestable; that we have moral senses of things without any pains or care taken to acquire them; that

they

they judge inftantaneoufly without our knowing why; and ftrike their notices upon us forcibly againft our utmoft endeavours to ftifle them. For by this rule our knowledge of language may be counted natural; because men in general have fome language; we learn our mother tongue without care or pains; the meaning of what we hear ftrikes us inftantaneoufly with the found, though we know not why the words table or chair, were affixed to the things they fignify; nor can we, with our utmoft endeavours, diffociate fcandal, or unwelcome truths from the expreffions conveying them.

Nor yet does he think their being derived from expedience any ways depreciates their value: for when our moral fenfes give their notices ftrong, it is an evidence, which ought not to be difregarded, that we ourfelves formerly, or other perfons before us, have found an expedience in the practices they recommend, though we may not at prefent difcern it. Therefore they deferve the fame refpect as a man, in whofe judgement we can fully confide, who fhould give his advifes, without laying before us the grounds whereon he founded them.

Thus if any body fhall take offence at the fuppofition of there being no immediate natural connection between tranfgreffion and punifhment, let it be made known to him that this does not invalidate the rules, nor influence of juftice: for the chain is often too long for us to bear in mind, which juftifies us in bringing the two ends to a contiguity they had not in nature. Many evil imaginations of the heart are harmlefs, unlefs as they give the mind an evil turn, productive of bad actions: many fingle deviations from rule may be innocent, otherwife than as they lead into pernicious habits: and in fome inftances an act of

injuftice

Demerit.

pathy[d], but whoever acquired them firſt, learned them by obſervation of their neceſſary injuſtice might be expedient, were it not for ſetting a bad example, or opening a door to licentiouſneſs in ourſelves, by throwing us off our guard upon other occaſions. Nor is it uncommon for men, after ſome years experience over their heads, to diſcern a fatal tendency in irregularities, it would have been impoſſible to have convinced them of in their youth. So that if we were never to proceed againſt offences without aſking, why, what harm do they do? we might not always be ready with an anſwer: and vice muſt go unpuniſhed, our own failings ſtand uncorrected, and the miſchiefs remotely conſequent thereupon muſt be incurred. Wherefore it is right, becauſe neceſſary, to make the tranſlation of odium to wickedneſs compleat, without which the connection could not be preſerved: and a prudent man will teach others, and enure himſelf, to feel an abhorrence of it upon no further view, than its blackneſs. Thus the aſſociation between Demerit and Depravity derives from prudence, not from nature: men being led into into it by the expedience there is in aſſociating them cloſely together without the intervention of expedience.

And in like manner he has laid down upon a former occaſion, that things deſerve honour, not merely becauſe they are uſeful, but becauſe it will be uſeful to place honour upon them.

[d] The ſubject of a ſeparate chapter. By this term, he underſtands that aptneſs we all have, more or leſs, of taking the ſentiments, the ideas, the affections, of the company we conſort with, and in general caſting our imagination into the ſame train with theirs: without

cessary tendency to good order and happiness, and by experience of the mischiefs resulting from those practises they would restrain. The frequent view of these good effects casts a value upon the sentiments producing them, and the translation being once compleatly made, desire fixes upon them as upon its ultimate object.

We find judgement does the same with respect to truth translated from the Postulata to the Problem demonstrated: the equality between the squares of the two sides and hypothenuse in a rectangular triangle serves, for a basis in mathematical and mechanical operations without our running back per-

out which conversation would grow languid, the pleasures of society lose their relish, and our inclination to good offices its vigour. This is another main spring of our motives, and even of our judgements; and performs its work much quicker than translation: for we do not presently drop our ends out of view, but we often imbibe desires and opinions from others in an instant.

The dexterous management of this engine makes a great part of the Poet's and Orator's arts, for upon it depends the efficacy of exclamation, positiveness, and ridicule, and of *Horace*'s rule, if you would have me weep, you must first be grieved yourself.

petually

petually through the whole procefs whereby *Euclid* convinced us of its being a truth. In like manner when our moral fenfes are grown vigorous, we follow their impulfe without thinking of any higher principle firft recommending them, and many of us without acknowledging any fuch principle.

Now I would not by any means leffen their influence, I rather wifh it were ftronger than it is; for we very feldom ftand in a fituation to difcern the expedience of our actions, nor where it lies any thing remote have we ftrength of mind enough to purfue it; but thefe moral fenfes ferve as excellent guides to direct, and fpurs to ftimulate us towards the attainment of a happinefs that would otherwife efcape us. Neverthelefs it muft be owned they partake of the nature of paffion, having the like qualities, the like vehemence and manner of operation, and may be ftiled virtuous appetites, as being the produce of reafon and induftry rather than of nature. They are to be ranked among the Scyons which *Plato* told us *Urania* grafted upon the

L wild

wild stocks in *Psyche*'s garden ᵉ, and which his master afterwards put us in mind were apt to run luxuriant, unless kept within bounds by a proper tendance.

Therefore it is one thing to consult our rules of action for shaping our conduct thereby, and another to examine the rules themselves for determining in what manner we shall establish, or rectify them. For as military discipline consists in the strict subordination of the soldiers to the officers,

---

ᵉ In his allegorical description of earthly and heavenly love, under the names of *Thalassian* and *Uranian* Venus, related in the Vision. He represents *Psyche* receiving her first notices from external objects and appetites, as she lay helpless in the garden of Nature. The gardener, *Selfish*, planted certain wild stocks producing crabbed fruits, until *Thalassio* grafted the accomplishments, and *Urania* the virtues upon them. The latter accompanied *Psyche* through the journey of life, and then setting her astride upon the golden anchor of *Elpis*, wafted her up into the blessed abodes.

Plato afterwards recounted some conversations he had formerly with a certain native of *Tarsus* in *Cilicia*, the substance of which he imparted to our Author; dressing them up after the philosophical manner. But unluckily our Author cannot recollect any thing at present; though he hopes to do it in convenient time, having some confused traces of them still in his memory.

and

and the officers to the general, so the little state of man is never so well disciplined as when the moral senses have the entire command of our motions, but lie themselves under controul of sober consideration and sound judgement. While in the hurry of action we have not leisure to consult the general, but must push bravely on whither our immediate officers lead us; nor indeed is consultation the business then, but intrepidity, vigour and alertness. Therefore the virtuous man acts because it is right and just, becoming and laudable, and forbears what appears wrong and base, unworthy and shocking to his thought: he follows the motions of zeal, honour, shame, decency, natural affection, civility, as he feels them rise in his breast; or if doubts arise he tries the moral senses by one another, and adheres to that which carries the strongest lustre, and highest excellency in his imagination, without considering further why he suffers himself to be guided by their influence, or whence it was derived. For the greatest part of mankind know not a *why* nor a *whence*, but take up their principles partly from their parents and tutors, partly from cuſtom and general eſtimation; and thoſe who do inveſtigate them to the fountain, cannot carry their inveſtigations in their head upon common occaſions.

But in ſeaſons of deliberation, when admitted into the general's tent, having the inſtructions and intelligences laid before us, and ſitting in council upon the operations of the campaign, it would be abſurd to take an officer's own teſtimonial of his merit, or give him his orders becauſe they are ſuch as he is moſt fond of executing; we are only to regard the public ſervice, what are each man's abilities, and how he may beſt conduct himſelf to promote it. So if we have ſufficient lights and opportunity to take our moral ſenſes under examination, in order to moderate what extravagancies they may have run into, or determine the rank among them in the command of our powers, it would be no leſs prepoſterous to try their rectitude by what themſelves ſuggeſt to be right, or to ſettle their degrees of authority

upon

Demerit.

upon any other foundation than their several tendencies towards the general happiness, wherein we shall always find our own contained.

§. 33. Now in matters of punishment, when we have it in our power, let us regard the heinousness of the offence, together with all circumstances that may aggravate or abate our abhorrence of it as beheld by our moral sense: but when we are to examine the foundation we have for entertaining this abhorrence, we shall find no other than the expedience [a] and necessity of pu-

[a] Were the connection between offence and punishment natural and necessary, there would be no room for mercy; for what nature has joined inseparably, the will of man ought not to put asunder, and what is odious in itself no circumstances can make innocent. But our rules of justice being imperfect, calculated for general use, and impossible to be adapted to every particular case, the exceptions whereto they are liable open the door to mercy: Which is not to be exercised arbitrarily, but guided by rules; such as the first offence, or the party being drawn in by surprize, or in hurry of passion, or upon repentance, which takes away the necessity of punishment, by answering the same purpose in preventing of future crimes. But mercy is as blamable as injustice, when extended without rule or reason, or perhaps unless when the rigour of the law, according to the vulgar saying, would be an injury.

nishment to preserve order, and good faith, and honesty among mankind. Even those who take private revenge, when called upon to justify their conduct, always plead that otherwise they should lie open to perpetual insults; which shews that the only reasonable excuse for resentment is not strictly the injury received, but the prevention of injuries for the future. Therefore reason, as well as authority, enjoins us to forgive our brother not only seven times, but until seventy times seven, unless where animadversion is necessary either for our own quiet and benefit, or that of others.

And there is a species of punishment called chastisement, which has no other object beside the benefit of the party upon whom it is exercised. Parents and schoolmasters may not be displeased at unlucky tricks played by their lads, as shewing a sagacity and sprightliness they delight to behold, yet they will not suffer them to pass with impunity, least it should generate idleness and other mischiefs: here is no abhorrence striking the moral sense, nor are the boys

boys difliked the worfe for their fallies of youth and ingenuity ill applied; fo the chaftifement is not for mifcarriages committed, but for future enormities which might be committed.

'Tis true the judge paffes fentence upon criminals by ftated rules, becaufe he is no more than a minifter to fpeak the fenfe of the law: but the legiflature, in eftablifhing the law, regards no other rules than thofe refpecting the public utility; therefore equal punifhments are appointed for offences of unequal enormity; for the law hangs for ftealing the value of five fhillings, but does no more for murder; and fome go wholly unpunifhed, fuch as ingratitude, intemperance, entailing difeafes or poverty upon families by gallantries or extravagance, becaufe they cannot be enquired into without caufing confufion and worfe inconveniencies. On the other hand, when the title to a throne is fo difputable that many honeft, well-difpofed perfons are drawn by mere error of judgment to take part on the unfortunate fide; they are adjudged and executed as rebels, becaufe it is neceffary to maintain the authority of government, and tranquillity of the state.

§. 34. Should it be objected, that this proves the contrary to what we have laid down, becaufe the law, whofe bafis is utility, does not govern us in our eftimation of Demerit, for we compaffionate inftead of detefting the deluded malecontent, while we acknowledge the expedience and neceffity of the law which condemns him, and think the abandoned debauchée deferving of punifhment which the law cannot provide for him; therefore we build our judgement upon other grounds than thofe of utility. I fhall anfwer, that as the law is not the fole meafure of juftice, fo neither is it the fole fountain of utility: for be the polity of a nation ever fo well regulated, or ever fo wifely adminiftered, the people muft ftill do fomething for themfelves in order to compleat their happinefs, and Providence has referved to his own management the putting a check upon fome enormities which the law cannot reach, nor human fagacity difcover or prevent.

Demerit.

Therefore that utility which the provisions of the law cannot totally compaſs, may ſtill remain for the foundation of private animadverſion and cenſure: nor is it a ſmall argument of its being ſo, that we naturally look upon the greatneſs of miſchief done as an aggravation of guilt in the perpetrator. If an unwholeſome potion be given to make a man ſick for a week, it is an injury; if it bring on an incurable diſeaſe, it is a more heinous offence; if death enſue, it is the crying ſin of murder.

Well, but you ſay the miſchief muſt be deſigned, or there will be no crime at all: the greater degree of miſchief is only an evidence of deeper blackneſs in the deſign; ſo that properly ſpeaking, it is not the damage done, but depravity of heart in the doer, which raiſes your abhorrence and wiſhes for vengeance; for when aſſured of the deſign, you pronounce the guilt the ſame, feel the ſame abhorrence and wiſh, although its purpoſe be utterly fruſtrated, and no damage at all enſue.

Why

Why this is the very thing I have been contending for all along, that the true ground of punishment is not the mischief done, or the crime committed, but the prevention of future enormities, productive of future mischiefs, and this object I think may fairly rank under the class of utility.

We have found in the former part of this work, that the volitions giving birth to our actions depend upon the present motives occuring to our thought, which are either what our judgement represents as most expedient, or our imagination as most alluring and desireable; and these motives are suggested by the opinions, the sentiments, the inclinations and habits we have contracted: when desire fixes upon practices of pernicious tendency, this is called a Depravity of Mind, or vulgarly, though improperly, a Depravity of Will, by a metonyme [a] of cause for effect, because the state

---

[a] Figures, though very convenient for common use, to give a lively tint to our ideas, and gain them an easy reception with those to whom we address ourselves, yet are dangerous things to the speculative, who

state of the mind, and desires in the heart, influence the will, and of course produce actions conformable thereto; for a good tree cannot bring forth evil fruit, neither can an evil tree bring forth good fruit.

Therefore this depravity of heart being productive of bad effects, whenever the season and opportunity serves to bring them to maturity, becomes justly odious upon account of the poisonous fruits it bears. But as punishment, animadversion and censure, being grievous to the party suffering them, tends to dissociate desire from the sentiments whereto they are annexed, and work amendment, or in other words, to give men a disgust for the vices rendering them obnoxious thereto; or at least to re-

who perplex themselves grievously by understanding figurative expressions literally. We have sufficiently seen the mischiefs of them in the difficulties upon Free-will, Election, and coexistent Powers, occasioned by taking the causes of volition, for volition itself. Those who use the common magnifying glass ordinarily puzzle themselves about the figure, without ever touching the thing signified, and make work enough for the genuine Microscope to rectify the blunders they commit.

strain

strain them from breaking forth into act, and discourage others from entertaining the like; it is this use which renders the punishment merited and just: for I appeal to any considerate person, whether he would punish, or ascribe to a depravity of heart any action, or sentiment whatever, which could never do the least hurt either to the owner, or any person in the world beside.

§. 35. For this reason freedom of action, and so much understanding as may make the party sensible for what the punishment was inflicted, are always esteemed necessary requisites to render him obnoxious thereto; because punishment operating upon the Imagination, and through that upon the Will, where either of these two channels are wanting, becomes useless, and consequently unjust. Therefore sly Revenges which may be mistaken for accidents, and nobody can know they were the effect of resentment, though sometimes practised by spiteful persons, have never been held warrantable by the judicious: nor will a righteous

ous man punish where the transgressor had not liberty of choice, nor where the reason of his punishing cannot be understood.

If a brick tumbles down upon you, it would be ridiculous to fall a whipping, or breaking it, because such discipline could contribute nothing towards preventing other bricks afterwards from tumbling upon your own, or somebody else's head; but had our treatment with brickbats any influence upon their future motions, we should form rules of justice for our dealings with them as well as with one another. When the puppy dog fouls your parlour you beat him for it; but then you rub his nose in the filth to make him sensible why he is beaten; and you think this severity justifiable, without discerning any depravity of heart in the beast, only because it secures your rooms against the like disaster for the future: but if he has stolen a woodcock from the larder, and you do not discover the theft till next morning, when your correction can do no good, it would be cruelty to chastise him.

Mischiefs

Mifchiefs done by mere accident are judged pardonable: but why? becaufe punifhment has no influence upon accidents: for in fome cafes, where better care may prevent them, we do not fcruple to animadvert in order to fpur men to greater vigilance: the ftatute of *Ann* lays a heavy penalty upon fervants fetting a houfe on fire undefignedly; nor did I ever hear that ftatute complained of as contrary to natural juftice.

Why are military punifhments feverer than all others? Is there greater depravity in difobedience to an officer, than to a civil magiftrate, a parent, or a mafter? Not fo, but becaufe the fervice requires a ftricter difcipline, and more implicit obedience. Nor can you pretend the foldiers confent upon enlifting, for many of them are inveigled to enlift by drink, or by the bounty-money, without knowing what they undertake, or confidering the rules they fubmit to: befides that you fubject the impreffed man to the fame feverities with the volunteer.

Demerit.

Why is the law of fashion so strict upon little matters, that a man would make himself more ignominious by wearing his wig the wrong side outwards, than by corresponding with the Pope, or the Pretender? unless because censure, exclamation and ridicule, being the only penalties you have to enforce it, you must lay them on the more lustily to keep the thoughtless world to decency in matters wherein they have no other restraint upon them.

Thus whatever species of punishment we fix our eye upon, we shall always find it deducible from utility; but the deduction is too long to carry constantly in our heads, nor can every head trace it out; neither do we upon all occasions stand in a situation to discern the consequences of our punishing, or sparing: therefore the judicious, from their observation of those causes, so far as they can investigate them, strike out rules of justice, and distinguish degrees of wickedness, which they hang up in public as marks, or erect as posts of direction to guide our steps in the journey of life, and
inculcate

inculcate a moral sense, or abhorrence of evil, to serve as a guard to protect us against inordinate desires that might tempt us to injustice, and as a measure to apportion our resentment against the heinousness of an offence, or depravity of an offender.

Such of us as are well disciplined look up to these marks continually, and shape their steps accordingly, both with respect to what they shall avoid themselves, and what notice they shall take of the proceedings and sentiments of their fellow-travellers, without thinking of any thing further; and much the greater part of us without knowing of any thing further to be thought of: when these latter get a smattering of philosophy, you hear them declaim incessantly upon the essential and unalterable rules [a] of right and wrong, independent

[a] It is difficult to conceive a rule not relating to the action of some Beings existent: for a rule respecting nonentities can scarce deserve the name of one. Therefore Rules can be no older than the Beings they relate to, nor have existence before these were created. Neither can they be independant on God, because depending upon the condition, wherein he placed his creatures.

Demerit.

dependent on God himself, having a nature he did not give them, and being an obligation upon him that he must not break through.

§. 36. But the all-seeing eye of God stretches wide and far, beholds all nature and all futurity in one unbounded prospect, therefore needs no marks nor rules [a] to direct his measures, nor moral senses to protect creatures. For if men had no property, there could be no such rule as, *Thou shalt not steal*; neither could there be a rule, *Thou shalt not bear false witness*, if men had not the use of speech. Our Author has considered this matter more at large in his chapter on Rectitude, where he has endeavoured to settle the proper import of essential and intrinsic, when applied thereto, and show how those words have been abused, by extending them to a latitude never thought of by such as first employed them.

[a] Nor virtues, nor passions, nor affections. Therefore when we say he is just or merciful, jealous, or compassionate, angry or grieved, or repentant; these are only so many forms whereinto we are forced to cast his wisdom, in order to bring it suitable to our conception. For when he pursues the like measures as we are prompted to by those affections, he does it upon a discernment of their propriety to effect his purposes. Which motive sometimes carries him in contrariety to these

against temptations which cannot approach him: for in every application of second causes, he bears his ultimate end constantly in view, and pursues it unerringly and invariably. What this end may be, perhaps it were in vain for us to enquire, but the utmost point beyond which we can conceive nothing further, is the good and happiness of his creatures: this then we must regard as the centre wherein all his dispensations terminate, and by the tendency whereto he regulates his measures of justice.

Now Punishment must be acknowledged an evil to the sufferer while under the lash of it, therefore unless we will suppose the fountain of Goodness sometimes to terminate his views upon evil, we must allow that he never punishes, unless for some greater benefit to redound therefrom, either to the offender, or some other part of the

these affections: for he suffers the wicked to pass with impunity, when he has any good to bring out of their evil, and the righteous to lie under distresses, when tending to work out a greater weight of glory for them.

creation.

Demerit.

creation. What other benefits may arise therefrom we know not, but we know its tendency to check or cure a depravity of heart where it is, to discourage the contracting of it where it is not, and consequently to prevent the mischievous fruits growing from that evil root.

Therefore as men are constituted, this remedy is necessary to restrain enormities from abounding among them, unless you will suppose a miraculous interposition, which is not the usual method of providence; and it is this necessity which justifies the punishment, and ascertains the measure of it. If we go on to enquire further, why men are so constituted, this will involve us in another question, which never was, and perhaps never will be determined by the sons of *Adam*, namely, why pain, distress, affliction, and uneasiness of all kinds, were permitted at all in the world; for moral evil were no evil if there were no natural; because, how could I do wrong, if no hurt or damage could ensue therefrom to any body, and is no greater than the

mis-

mischiefs whereof it may be productive? Therefore it is natural evil which creates the difficulty, and the quantity of this evil is the same from whatever causes arising. "Think ye those eighteen upon whom the tower in *Siloam* fell were sinners above all other *Galileans?*" We are told, nay: yet the pain, the loss of life, and other damages they sustained, were the same in quantity as if they had brought down the ruin upon their own heads by their misconduct.

Let any man explain to me clearly how the permission of mischievous accidents is consistent with our ideas of infinite goodness, and I will undertake to show him by the lights he shall afford me, how the permission of moral evil is likewise consistent. The only solution of this difficulty I apprehend must be taken from the imperfection [b] of our understanding, for we have

ob-

---

[b] Our Author in his chapter on Goodness, supposes some other Attribute, unknown to the sons of *Adam*, to set the bounds to infinite Goodness, that it may not be coextensive with Omnipotence. And in a discourse he had with an angel in the vision, on his return

Demerit.

observed in a former place, that infinite Goodness and infinite Power considered in the abstract, seem incompatible [c]: which shows there is something wrong in our conceptions, and that we are not competent judges of what belongs, and what is repugnant to goodness. But God knows though we do not, and is good and righteous

---

turn back from the mundane soul into the vehicular state, he is shown that there must be other attributes besides those whereof we have any conception, because these would not suffice for the business of the Creation.

Dacier would have said, he took this hint from *Moses* being admitted to see the back parts of God, but not his whole person. But *Search* assures me, he thought nothing of *Moses* while he was with the angel. He had indeed before taken notice of the expression, that no man can see God and live; which he expounded, not that the sight would be so terrible as to destroy us, but that man, while imprisoned in this mortal body, has not faculties to discern the divine Nature, and so cannot see God while he lives under this veil of flesh.

[c] Because our idea of infinite Goodness seems to require, that it should exhaust Omnipotence, and our idea of the latter, that it should be inexhaustible. Since then we find something wrong in our conceptions, how can it be expected we should explain an object we have not faculties to comprehend? Therefore our want of understanding is no proof against its reality.

in all his ways; therefore whatever method he purfues is an evidence of its rectitude beyond all other evidences that can offer to us for the contrary.

§. 37. Juftice regards folely the degree of depravity exiftent, nor has any concern with the manner how it came to exift: a man bribed with a large fum of money is not excufed by the guilt of the employer, although perhaps he would never have thought of committing the crime without that temptation; and if evil communication corrupts good manners, the corruption coming through this channel does not exempt it from cenfure. The perpetration indeed of villainies, without any inftigation or inducement, aggravates their heinoufnefs, becaufe it indicates a greater depravity of heart; but the degree of depravity once afcertained, always fets the meafure to the deteftation and demerit of the offender, without enquiring into the fource from whence it was derived; and

we

Demerit.

we shall find it so in whatever case we consider maturely and candidly.

Suppose you and I delegated by heaven to govern some little district, with absolute power of life and death over the inhabitants, with perfect knowledge of the secrets of their hearts, and were sitting in council together upon the measures of executing our commission, which we were resolved to do with exact justice and integrity. Suppose further, what has been shown not to be the real fact, but in order to make our case the stronger for our present purpose, let us suppose that men had been hitherto utterly destitute of Freewill, but guided in all their motions by an external influence; and their sentiments and dispositions thrown upon them, without their own act, by the impulse of necessary causes; but at the moment when we entered upon our office, this influence and impulse were taken off, and they were put into the condition of common men, whom we have conversed with in the world: how should we proceed to manage with them.

In the first place it may be presumed we should agree upon a general amnesty for the past, in consideration of the force they had lain under; and in the next, we should contrive measures for their future well-being, and finding them in possession of powers of action, together with liberty to use them, we should study to turn their Freewill into courses most advantageous to the community. If we saw vices and malignancy among them, we might probably feel an abhorrence and detestation thereof, for I do not suppose ourselves divested of the moral senses we had acquired before, but this sentiment would be like that aversion we have to spiders, toads and adders, who did not make themselves what they are, but received their venom and ugliness from the hand of nature; yet I hope we should be too equitable to punish any man merely because we did not like his looks, unless where those looks manifested a badness of heart, productive of mischief to himself or his neighbours, and then we should apply such punishments, notes of infamy,

Demerit.

infamy, or censures, as we judged most proper for preventing his ill qualities from breaking forth into act, or spreading the contagion elsewhere, thinking our proceedings justifiable by their expedience, and regulating the measure of our punishments by their several aptness to answer the purpose intended.

§. 38. If then we find that human reason, when acting most conformably to our ideas of prudence and equity, would restrain depravity, from whatever sources arising, by adequate punishments, why should we arraign the justice of God for proceeding in the like manner? For he beholds the works of his hands, and discerns whereof they are made, nor is he unacquainted with the operations and uses of second causes: He has made moral evil the general, and, as some believe, the sole * fountain of natural

---

* It is a very orthodox tenet, that pain and misery were brought into the world, as well among the brute as the rational creation, by the fall of *Adam*. And the ancient Mythologists give us a description of their golden

ral: He has given man freedom to choose between good and evil: He knows that
· · · · · · · vices

golden age, similar to that of paradise, exempt from both evils. Yet though they have made the moral coeval with the natural, they seem not to have supposed them effects of one another; but both co-effects of the same cause, to wit, the gradual decay of nature in her three changes, from the golden age to the silver, from silver to brass, and from thence to iron. The Philosophers appear to have held natural evil the consequence of moral; which opinion we may suppose they founded upon the divine Goodness, from whence nothing evil could proceed, but the creatures brought it upon themselves by the perverse use of their powers. But then they conceived this attribute must require, that the natural evil should result from the moral of that particular creature upon whom it fell: for they could not understand it consistent with goodness that any one should suffer for the failings of another. This led them into the notion of a pre-existent state, wherein every man, by his misbehaviour, may have rendered himself obnoxious to the misfortunes he undergoes in the present.

I need not remark the absurd consequences that would follow from this doctrine supported upon these grounds: which must with equal reason infer a preexistence for the brute creation too, down to the pismire, the maggot, the new-found polypus, and scarce-perceptible puceron he devours, together with a rationality therein, rendering them capable of moral good and evil. Because though we can account for the distresses of men, the maimed and distempered births

of

vices will abound among them, which will influence them to use their freedom to pernicious

of children, from the derivation of original sin: yet that sin being never extended to the animals, will not account for the sufferings brought upon them by their tyrannical lord, imperial man, by their fellow subjects, by weather, or accidents. I say, I need not urge this objection, the doctrine of Pre-existence being now universally exploded. For every old woman knows the soul of the child was created at the very instant when the mother first felt herself quick. And any body may see with half an eye, that if we had all existed a hundred years ago, some or other of us must have remembered it. Besides, if we would not beat a dog, unless for some fault he may be sensible of, who can imagine we should be punished ourselves, without letting us know for what? But the most solid argument against Pre-existence arises from its uselessness: for what is past and gone we have nothing to do with, our concern lies only with the future, and it behoves us to shape our behaviour in such manner as may make our condition happy hereafter. If we could demonstrate our Pre-existence ever so clearly, we could not expect to know what passed with us in that state, nor gather from thence a fund of experience whereon to build observations for regulating our future conduct. Therefore this subject is not worth our taking into consideration at all; and without considering, we can see no proofs of its reality; and without proofs it would not become us to believe it; and what does not become us to believe, there can be no harm in running down with exclamation or ridicule. The like may be said of the

Pre

nicious purposes, and has appointed punishment as one of the springs to operate upon Pre or Post-existence of animals, which if we could discover, would neither do us any service, nor enable us to do them any. And the same method might be proper in other cases, by refusing to puzzle our thoughts with curious speculations, which if investigated to the utmost can do no good.

Nor would our author be displeased to have it practised upon himself: for there are things useful to some, which are not so, but rather mischievous to others; and he has been forced sometimes to enter upon subjects that might scandalize the scrupulous, or hurt the unwary, to whom he hopes to give better content, when he can recover the matters before mentioned to have been communicated by *Plato* from the *Cilician*: but this must be a work of time. In the mean while, he would be glad that every one would follow him in the discussion of such points as they find suited to their taste or liking, passing lightly over the rest, as the wanton rovings of a speculative fancy. For my friend *Search*, to do him justice, has an honest heart, and would willingly give offence to nobody, but dispense his wares about in quarters where they might at least be harmless. But, as he has observed in a discourse upon this topic with his vehicular conductor, the antients, delivering their lectures by word of mouth, could adapt their subjects to their audience, reserving their esoteries for adepts, and dealing out exoteries only to the vulgar: whereas we moderns having no other channel of communication than the press, must throw out both sorts to the mercy of every man that can raise the pence to buy a copy, or has a friend of whom he can borrow one.

the

Demerit.

the human mind for reftraining the growth of wickednefs, and preventing its bad effects. Can we then doubt that he will employ all the fprings of action in thofe ufes, and upon thofe occafions wherein he in his wifdom judges them refpectively proper? or what rule of juftice does he violate by fo doing?

Why he permitted moral evil, is a confideration quite foreign to the prefent fubject, and can only produce that entanglement naturally confequent upon blending difcuffions of different natures together: for whether we can reconcile that permiffion with our ideas, or no, ftill evil being once permitted, becomes a foundation for juftice to ward off the bad effects that might enfue from it: for juftice cannot ftand at variance with goodnefs, nor can one ever forbid what the other recommends.

As the judge paffes fentence upon the houfe-breaker and the affaffin, not in animofity to them, but in regard to the honeft man, that he may fleep quietly in his bed, and go about his lawful occafions without

hazard

hazard of his life: fo God punifhes the wicked not in wrath and deteftation, but in mercy and loving-kindnefs, many times to the delinquent himfelf, but always either to him or his fellow-creatures.

Therefore to the queftion, Who hath ever refifted his will? Why then doth he punifh? It may be anfwered, To fecure the further accomplifhment of his will, and to effect his gracious purpofes towards thofe whom he intended to preferve from the like wickednefs, or the pernicious confequences fpringing therefrom: views wherein we cannot find the leaft tincture of injuftice or arbitrary proceedings.

§. 39. But it is not enough to juftify the ways of God, unlefs we endeavour likewife to obviate the perverfe confequences men fometimes draw from the will of God being conftantly fulfilled. For, fay they, if that will always take place, then we have no will of our own, being pinned down to one particular manner of proceeding, which it is his will fhould be taken.

But

Demerit.

..But if human action were necessary, as indeed it is not, we have seen that would not excuse iniquity from punishment, as being an application of the proper cause for preventing the growth and mischiefs of it; and this persuasion sufficiently inculcated, would necessarily, if the operation of motives be necessary, drive them into a course of thinking and acting productive of happiness; and if they attain the possession of this treasure, 'tis not much matter whether they apprehend themselves procuring it by necessary or voluntary agency [c]: therefore they
will

---

[c] 'Squire *Search* in this place probably had a view to the dispute that happened upon the road some time ago between him and Doctor *Hartley*. The squire, it seems, in his chapter on the causes of action, had assigned the mind herself for the efficient cause of all we do: this the doctor would not allow; for he gave the following account of the matter. The human body, says he, is a collection of little threads or fibres curiously bound up together; among which the Ether insinuates throughout every part of our frame, disposing itself into strings running cross-wise between the sides of the interstices wherein it lies. When objects strike upon our senses, they agitate the fibres of the organ whereon they fall: which agitation puts the etherial strings contiguous to them into little tremours, called

will do well to contemplate the penalties annexed to evil-doing; for it will do them good one way or other, if not as exhortation to work upon a free agent, at least as a salutary medicine to rectify the disorders in their machine.

But

called by him Vibratiuncles. As the strings communicate with one another all over our body, the foresaid vibratiuncles excite others correspondent to them in the strings lying about the nerves of our muscles, thereby agitating those nerves, which produce a contraction in the muscles, and cause them to move the limbs. The tremours in the first mentioned strings he stiles sensory vibratiuncles, and in the latter motory vibratiuncles. Thus the doctor acknowledges all human action necessary, being performed by the mechanical running of vibratiuncles from the sensory to the motory, without any intervention of the mind to assist in the operation. He allows indeed that the vibratiuncles, in their passage, touch at the seat of the mind, where they leave information of the way they are going, and of the external objects exciting them. so the mind, having continual notice of what is doing, fancies herself the author of all that is done; whereas in reality she sits an idle spectator only, not an agent of our actions; like the fly upon the chariot-wheel, ascribing to her own prowess, the mighty clouds of dust she sees raised around her.

Now, my cousin *Search* not having studied anatomy, thought himself no match at argument for the learned physician, so declined entering the lists with him, but

pro-

Demerit.

But an event being agreeable to the will of another, does not always hinder it from being the choice of our own will too: what I do by the command of a superior, while I pay him a chearful and ready obedience, is done by the will of both. 'Tis lucky, you

proposed a feigned issue to be tried by the country, in imitation of those directed out of chancery, upon the following case. Mr. *Jeffery Dolittle,* a gentleman of tolerable capacity and good repute among his neighbours, departed this life in an unusual manner; for one morning after breakfast his perceptive or spiritual part was taken from him miraculously, without any disease, disorder, accident, or dislocation of any single particle either in the grosser or finer part of his material frame. The question is, how this defunct or mere machine would behave? Both parties agree, that the pulse would continue to beat, the lungs to play, the animal secretions to be carried on, the vibratiuncles to traverse to and fro, as before, and that by dinner-time the tongue and palate might come into that state which affects us with hunger; yet the perceptive mind being gone, there would be no uneasiness for want of victuals, nor perception of the objects round about. But *Search,* in his declaration, avers, that it would not walk down stairs, sit down to table, carve the meats, converse with the company, nor give its opinion upon the conduct of the ministry, usefulness of the militia, or whether *Nivernois* comes in good earnest to conclude, or only to amuse us. The doctor in his plea insists, that it would do all this, and every thing else
that

you say, I stand so disposed, for I must have done the thing had I been ever so desirous of the contrary: so I am in the condition of a man sitting in a room where the doors are locked upon him without his perceiving it; he is actually a prisoner, though

that might be expected from a reasonable creature, and well-bred gentleman. And upon this point issue was joined.

But it being difficult presently to impanel a jury who would consent to be shut up without victuals, drink, or candle, until they should agree upon a verdict, the litigants struck up a compromise in the mean time, that each should jog on his own way without interruption from the other. For, says *Search*, I suppose, doctor, we both aim at doing some good to mankind by our labours: now if we can effect our purpose, 'tis not a farthing matter by what process the operation goes on. Whether we can draw such scratches upon paper, as that the rays reflected therefrom shall raise vibratiuncles in the reader, which shall inform him of salutary theorems, that will better the condition of his mind, and beget motory vibratiuncles that will put his limbs into a course of action most conducive to his benefit; or whether, by the ordinary methods of conviction, instruction, and exhortation, we can spur him on to use his own activity in a manner most beneficial to himself.

Pursuant to this compromise, we see in the text before us, that our author, so he can work a persuasion productive of happiness, does not care whether it operates by free or necessary agency.

he

he does not feel his confinement, becaufe he happens to choofe the only thing in his power, that is, to ftay where he is.

But what if I do a good office for an acquaintance to whom I owe no obligation, nor have other inducement than good nature? do not I gratify his will and my own at the fame time? Or what if an artful politician, who can fee through and through me, leads me dextroufly to co-operate with his defigns: although the iffue fhould fall out befide or contrary to my intention, ftill the fteps I am made to take by his management were the work of my own will. So when God puts in ufe the proper caufes for producing an event, we need not fear but he will adapt them fo wifely as that they fhall not fail to accomplifh his will; neverthelefs, if among thefe caufes there be the motives fit to work upon a free agent, the act performed is as compleatly the will of that agent, as if his ideas had derived from any other fource, or been thrown up by the fortuitous declination of *Epicurus*'s atoms.

Demerit.

The fallacy here lies in the same equivocation of language taken notice of in the foregoing pages, to which I refer any body who thinks it needful to revise what has been already offered: for the Will of God must be fulfilled in no other sense than what was absolutely foreknown, or contained in the plan of Providence; must come to pass, not by compulsion or necessity, but by removal of all hazard to the contrary.

§. 40. Another fond imagination may start up in men's heads from the never-failing completion of the divine Will, as if it justified them in all the follies they have been guilty of; for, say they, whatever we have done must have been agreeable to the Will of God, because having taken effect; for nothing has fallen out that was not so; therefore wherein have we done amiss? for who hath ever resisted his Will? And they put this question by way of defiance, to give any other than one certain answer.

But

But they deceive themselves by their manner of wording the queſtion; for had it been aſked, who hath defeated his Will? we could not have produced an inſtance, nor yet would it have ſerved their purpoſe, nor furniſhed an excuſe for their miſconduct that we could not: but who hath reſiſted his Will? is no ſuch unanſwerable queſtion; for the Will may be reſiſted without ſucceſs, and then come to paſs notwithſtanding; or it may be miſunderſtood, and in that caſe accompliſhed by the very endeavour to do ſomething contrary to it.

Suppoſe you lend money to a friend upon his note; he being at a diſtance, and fully confiding in your honour, ſends you a letter with the value incloſed, only deſiring you will burn the note, that your executors may not find it to charge him with the debt; but before you can fulfill his requeſt, ſomebody elſe finds the note, who having a ſpite againſt you, throws it into the fire with intention to diſable you from recovering the ſum contained in it; here he acts in direct oppoſition to your Will, his deſign is nothing else than to cross and thwart you; yet in so doing he does the very thing you will should be done, and would have done yourself, if he had not been beforehand with you. In like manner we may, and too frequently do, resist the Will of God, but by that very resistance accomplish it; for we act in the dark, scarce ever knowing what is his real Will, or that, its constant aim, the good of his creation; with the greatest part whereof we have no visible connection, nor the least suspicion of what concern their interests have with our proceedings.

We have often heard of a distinction between the secret [a], and declared Will, the

---

[a] Great mischiefs and much enthusiasm have arisen in the world, from pretending to pry into the secret Will. The very attempt is highly absurd; for can we fancy ourselves wiser than God, or cunning enough to find out what he purposely conceals? Therefore we are constantly to esteem that his Will, to which we are directed by the rules assigned us, or lights afforded us: nor can any thing else be counted such until verified by the event, and that will not justify our having proceeded to accomplish it. For though whatever has been permitted, was best to be done, because Providence

the latter is so much as we can discover by the best use of our understanding, which being fallible, will sometimes discover to us what is not the truth; yet this is the guide God has given us for our direction, and while we act conformably thereto,

dence orders all things for the best; yet is this no plea for the transgressor: because the merit of an action depends upon the ultimate point in view: whatever lies beyond, which could not be discerned, has no share in the estimation.

Tully relates a story of one *Jason* of *Phereu*, who had an impostume upon his stomach, that could not be cured by any means or assistance he could procure. It became so troublesome to him, that he grew tired of life; but having not learned the stoical doctrine of Suicide, he determined to dispose of his life for the benefit of his country; so he entered into the wars, and put himself foremost in all dangerous enterprizes. In one of these he received a wound with a spear, which luckily opened the impostumation, and worked a perfect cure. Now had this wound been given in private enmity instead of open war, every body would have condemned it as a crying enormity. For the intention whereon the view terminates, must denominate the deed: and though it was the Will of God to restore health and ease by this means to the sufferer, yet this object lying out of sight could have no effect to brighten the colour of the action. Nor could the Perpetrator be said to do the Will of God, because he acted in disobedience to his declared Will, contained in the command, *Thou shalt do no murder*.

although

although the event by disappointing our endeavours should prove the secret Will to have been otherwise, nevertheless our honest, though mistaken zeal for his service, will stand approved in his sight, and engage his bountiful favour towards us.

Whereas on the other hand, if we perversely run counter to the admonitions of this guide, it will avail us nothing that our being permitted to take our course proves it agreeable to the secret Will; for God does not punish in anger, nor for having been disappointed of his purpose; a cause of resentment which can never befall him; but with the view of a physician who prescribes a smart operation necessary to cure a distemper that would destroy the patient, or infect the neighbourhood: and if we regard our vicious dispositions in this light, which is the true one, we must behold them with the same aversion we should a loathsome disease, whether we apprehend it brought upon us by our own mismanagement, or inflicted by the hand of heaven; which aversion once become hearty and strong,

strong, may be trusted to take its chance for the effect it will have upon our conduct.

§. 41. For it is not so material to give a right judgement upon what is past and cannot be undone, as to take right measures for the future. Therefore left any should encourage themselves in indolence, or wrong doing, under pretence that since the Will of God is always punctually fulfilled, whatever shall be done, good or bad, must be conformable to that Will, so they need not scruple to take the courses they like, being sure to accomplish it at all events: let them consider, that since that Will shall take effect at all events, they may as well accomplish it by doing right, as wrong, being equally sure either way, that what they shall do will be the thing that was to come to pass; if then the Will of God be done in both cases, and they have their choice [a] in what manner they shall accomplish

[a] For we may place the matter in this light, as having it in our option, with respect to events within our power, to determine what shall be the Will of God.

If

plish it, had they not better choose the manner most advantageous to themselves, than one pernicious and destructive to them?

For If at any time we can know the tendency of all causes in act, we may know what is the Will of God in that instance: therefore where the powers of men are those causes, we may know that Will, by knowing the turns that human volition shall take; and wherever we can, by our resolves, give the turn to our own volition, God leaves us at liberty to determine his Will. Nor is there greater absurdity in this thought, than in conceiving a mother permitting her child to determine which way she shall lead him, or a king his deserving subject what title of honour he shall confer upon him.

Suppose a man says to me, I got drunk last night; therefore it was the Will of God, because done. Indeed I was bloody sick this morning: but then it was best I should be so, because finding a place in the plan of Providence. Very well; but is this a reason why you should get drunk again to night? For if you keep sober, that will likewise be God's Will: and if you have no qualms to-morrow, that will be the best, because obtaining a place in the same plan. Since then either way will conduct you surely to that ultimate best known only to God, why should you not take the cleanest, safest road, rather than involve yourself in the filth and dangers of debauchery? Nor were the case different could you swallow ever so much without being sick or sorry: for the notices of your moral sense,

Demerit.

For our bufinefs is to purfue our own trueft interefts; we have nothing to do with the fecret Will; that will work itfelf out without our follicitude to compleat it: the end affigned us to work out, is none other than our own happinefs, to be purfued carefully and induftrioufly, according to the lights afforded us.

Good and evil lie before us; we have powers of action, with liberty to ufe them: if our powers at any time be limited, we have ftill fome fcope to range in; if our paffions, or evil habits abridge our liberty, ftill we may ftrive and ftruggle againft them: in all cafes there is fomething or other wherein we may exert our endeavours; let us then apply them where they may turn moft to our benefit; but above

fenfe, and the judgement of confiderate perfons diffuading excefs, are an evidence you have reafon to confide in, for the reality of mifchiefs you may not immediately difcern. So you have no concern with that Will which is verified only by the event, but may confult your own liking; provided you do not confine your regards to your prefent liking, but extend them to the confequences, which you may vehemently diflike.

all

all beware of reducing ourselves to such a deplorable condition, as that even mercy and loving-kindness must lay a heavy weight of punishment upon us in order to effect its gracious purposes.

Fate. §. 42. There is still another quarter of the wilderness we have not yet explored, where the giant Fate stalks along with irresistable strides, bearing down the forrest like tender blades of corn before him, forcing his passage through ramparts and rocks; the textures of human contrivance are but as the dewy cobwebs of autumn across his way; nor can Freewill find a place for the sole of her foot among the heapy ruins wherewith he bestrews the ground[a].

But

---

[a] Upon my friend's showing me this transition, I recollected that a little before we had read together the poems of *Ossian* the son of *Fingal*. I told him I thought here was an instance of that sympathy he has talked of so much, as being one principal channel by which we daily furnish our imagination with motives, affections, sentiments, and trains of thought. I know, says I, the star from whence you catched this spark of

the

Fate.

But before we enter into an examination of the courses of Fate, let us, according to our usual custom, endeavour to understand what is properly meant by the word. We find it often confounded with Necessity,

or

the sublime. Of the Pompeus rather, says he. But when we take a fresh sympathy, it is apt to hang loose upon us like *Horace*'s purple rag, until incorporated in time among the old trains.

These sympathies, cousin *Comment*, are helpful to form and improve the stile: and it is necessary to store in variety of them from different quarters, or else we shall be servile copiers instead of bold imitators. You are right, cousin *Search*, says I. But may not this variety be multiplied too far? For where will you find readers with the like variety of tastes? And you have laid down, that when the trains suggested to an auditor are so dissimilar to those he has been accustomed to that they cannot possibly run into one another, it generates antipathy instead of sympathy. But as you have managed the matter, there is nobody who will not find something to excite this antipathy. The grave will be disgusted to see you handle the most serious subjects in the air of a novel or a comedy: and the gay will find themselves grievously disappointed, when you draw them by the lure of amusement into a metaphysical subtilty. And you know that what nauseates, hangs longer upon the palate than what is suitable to the taste. So that by aiming to please every body, you will please nobody: because there is nobody who will not think you either too profound or

too

or the impulsive operation of necessary causes: so the *Stratonic* and *Democratic* Atheists [b] understood it, when they ascribed all

too playfull. Your remark, says he, Cousin, is just, provided I were to consult Reputation only. But who knows but that by blending the airy and the abstruse, I may show the contemplative that it is possible to be serious without being solemn, to pursue inventions without injury to truth, and give a loose to imagination without losing one's understanding: and if I have carried matters beyond bounds, they may proceed with better discretion. On the other hand, by flourishing about and pretending to amuse, I may bring the thoughtless unawares into a closeness of thinking, which they used to dread, as being incompatible with chearfulness.

Thus the conversation ended, as conversations generally do, each party retaining his own opinion.

[b] They held atoms eternal and uncreated; and out of these, by their various collisions, assortments, and adhesions, the souls of men, and all other productions were formed. *Strato* made his atoms sentient, but in the lowest degree, so as not to be capable of a compleat perception; yet that a multitude of them clubbing forces might produce the brightest Genius or ablest Politician.

Our Author has battled both these people, showing that Perception cannot be made up of what are no Perceptions; nor received by a number of atoms jointly, unless received entire by each of them singly. For a sound cannot be heard by a whole assembly, without being heard by every one of the persons composing

Fate.

all events to Fate, that is, the actions of matter depending upon one another in a continued series from all eternity: and *Homer*'s *Moira crataia*, strong-handed fate, has been generally translated by the *Latin* poets, *dura Necessitas*, inflexible Necessity.

posing it: neither can whispers heard by a thousand men, make together an audible voice. He observes further, that existence belongs only to individuals; a compound being a number, or collection of substances, and having no other existence than that of its parts. For if the king were to incorporate six hundred men into a regiment, there would not be six hundred and one Beings therefore, one for the regiment, and one for each of the men, instead of only six hundred there were before; nor were he to break it again would their be a Being the less in his kingdom. So neither when a multitude of atoms run together to compose a human body, is there a Being more than there was before: nor would there be a Being lost out of nature upon its dissolution. But no man can doubt of his own existence, or that he has a personality belonging to him distinct from all other Beings: for I can never cease to be myself, nor become another person. Therefore there is one Being the more in nature for my existence; and were I annihilated there would be a Being the less. From hence he infers the individuality of the mind, or spirit of man, and consequently its perpetual duration: for nature can only destroy compounds by dissolving their parts, but individuals cannot be destroyed without a miracle, that is, an immediate exertion of Omnipotence.

But

But I conceive thefe two very different things in common underftanding, if we may reckon Neceffity as here ufed a common idea, for I rather take neceffary agency to be terms belonging to the fpeculative vocabulary; but apprehend that operations whereto they may be applicable, cannot upon that account be ftiled the work of Fate, in propriety of language. The circulation of fap in vegetables, the contraction and dilatation of their fibres, the action of the fun, air and mould, contributing to make them yield their feveral fruits, are all neceffary agencies: yet when a man plants a peach-tree, can you properly fay it is therefore fated that he fhall gather peaches and not plumbs or filberds therefrom; or if he fows oats in his field, does he think any thing of a fatality againft his reaping wheat or barley? So neither if we knew a collection of atoms having motions among them which muft form a regular world, fhould we efteem every thing

thing fatal [c] that might be produced by them.

But Fate, derived from the *Latin, Fari,* signifying to speak, must denote the word spoken by some intelligent Being, who has power to make his words good; so that whatever he says shall be done, will infallibly come to pass; and does not at all relate to the causes or manner whereby it is accomplished, unless those causes be made to act in consequence of the word spoken.

As to the *Parcæ,* supposed in heathen mythology to spin the thread of life, and by their scissars to determine the period of it, I should understand this thread only to express the series of events befalling every man, not the series of causes operating to bring them forth. And the Pagans seem unsettled in their notions concerning the author of 'Fate; sometimes it is their Jove who fixes it by his arbitrary decree, as in the ill successes of the *Grecian* army;

---

[c] Yet *Chrysippus, Seneca,* and the Stoics, speak in this stile, thereby extending the word to a sense not belonging to it in common language.

sometimes he is only an executive power, subordinate to the *Parcæ*, compelled by their spinning, to do or permit what he does not like, as in the death of *Sarpedon*[d].

However, leaving them to their own imaginations, with us who acknowledge one supreme Governour subordinate to nothing nor controulable by any other Power, Fate or Destiny, must be the same with the decree of the Almighty; nor can we doubt that whatever he has decreed will not fail of coming to pass.

§. 43. But this decree works no effect of itself, being no efficient cause; for if you order your servant to do a thing, the business is done by the efficacy of his action, not of your's; a command given to a subordinate, we shall acknowledge com-

---

[d] And sometimes himself subjected to their laws: for we learn from *Ovid*, that he remembered a time in the bosom of fate, wherein the sea, the earth, and imperial palace of heaven should be wrapt in flames: Yet it seems he knew so little the certainty of that time, that he was afraid the madness of *Phaeton* might anticipate it.

pulsive;

Fate.

pulsive; therefore if any man knows of a decree issued from the Almighty concerning something he is to do, I shall never advise him to strive against it, nor think himself at liberty to do the contrary.

But it is not this kind of decrees that are supposed to generate Fatality, which arises from those unknown to us, confining our actions to the course suited for bringing forth the destined event: yet even in this case it is not the word spoken and never heard by us, but something consequent upon it that imposes the Fatality. We are told indeed, that God said, *Let there be Light, and there was Light*; yet we cannot imagine the Light sprung forth without some exertion of Omnipotence to produce it; for when afterwards he said, *Let us make man after our own image*, nevertheless man was not made until he moulded the dust of the earth into a human body, and breathed thereinto the breath of life: therefore when we say God created all things by his word, we do not understand that they produced themselves out of non-entity,

entity, in obedience to the order given [a], but intend only to exprefs the facility wherewith the divine operations are performed fimilar to that of a man in authority, caufing what he pleafes to be done upon the word of command.

Very true, you fay: nobody imagines the found of words fpoken can work any thing. But when God pronounces his decree, he accompanies it with fome act of power efficacious and irrefiftible to enforce the execution: or he watches over the tendency of fecond caufes, and turns them by his fecret influence to co-operate towards bringing forth the deftined event: in both cafes he abridges human liberty; for what is ordained muft inevitably come to pafs; nor can all the art or power of man turn it afide; for the Fatality hanging over us confines our choice to one certain train of objects, or by privately counteracting us, baffles our utmoft endeavours, when turned the contrary way.

[a] Nor that this order was an efficient caufe of their exiftence.

§. 44. This seems to be the ordinary way of confidering this matter, and the concomitant exertion of power makes the difference between a Decree and a Command, for both are fuppofed to proceed from the word of God. We are told, he faid, *Let there be Light, and there was light*: we are likewife told, that he faid, *Thou fhalt not murther; thou fhalt not fteal; thou fhalt not commit adultery*; neverthelefs men do ftill murder and fteal, and commit adultery, notwithftanding the word fpoken. So the word of God operates nothing of itfelf when delivered as a command, nor unlefs when delivered as a decree: becaufe in the latter cafe only, it is accompanied with an exertion of Omnipotence, or a determination to exert it when occafion fhall require.

But the idea of a determination, to ufe power whenever requifite for accomplifhing a decree, arifes from our narrow conception of the proceedings of God taken from our own manner of proceeding, as obferved already in §. 20. and the latter part of §. 29. For when we resolve upon the compassing of any distant purpose, we can scarce ever lay our measures so surely but that they may fail of the issue intended; so we are forced to watch over and correct them from time to time as we shall find occasion; or accidents may intervene which will require our further endeavours to prevent their defeating our design; or many times we know not what measures are proper until we have seen the tendency of other causes, and conduct of other persons any ways affecting the end we have in view; and then we must employ such power and skill as we are masters of, in order to bring things into the train we would have them take. From this experience of ourselves, we are led to think the same of the Almighty, whom we conceive as having destined certain particular events, but in general left the powers of nature and free agents to take their own course, until they chance to take a tendency contrary to his designs, and then he controuls and turns them

them by his secret influence, so as to make them co-operate therewith.

Now a little reflection may show how injurious this notion is to the wisdom and power of God, representing him as fixing indeed upon certain purposes, but uncertain in what manner they shall be brought to pass, until the tendency his second causes shall happen to take points out the measures necessary for turning them into their destined course; and thus giving chance a share in the government of the world, liable indeed to his controul, but working of herself whenever he does not interfere, and even furnishing employment for his wisdom and power, by the errors she commits.

§. 45. But when we consider, that all events, as well those esteemed fortuitous as others, must proceed from certain causes, which derived their existence and efficacy mediately or immediately from the first; and when we contemplate his Omniscience, extending to every thing that can be supposed the object of knowledge, we shall find reason to convince us that nothing comes to pass unless in consequence of some act of his; and that whenever he acts, he knows precisely what he does, together with the remotest and minutest consequences to result from his doings.

For what bounds shall we set to his intelligence? If our own lies confined within a small compass, it is owing to the scantiness of our organs, those necessary instruments of our perception. We have but two hands, so can touch no more than they will reach to; we have eyes only before us, so can behold no further than half the circle surrounding us: the tablet of our memory, the chart of our imagination, the line of our reflection, have their appointed measures, so we can recollect, or calculate, or contemplate no more than the ideas they contain.

But God perceives not by organs, neither meditates by animal spirits, or the little fibres of the brain, nor receives his notices by channels, whose number or contents might

might be computed, so as to determine the precise quantity they are capable of conveying. What then is there to set the limitation to his knowledge; or by what rule or measure can we ascertain the bounds? Can he comprehend a million of ideas, and no more? Does he clearly discover all events to happen within the ensuing century, and no longer? Do the concerns of empires so occupy his thoughts, that he has none to spare for the peasant, the labourer, or the beggar? Are the affairs of men so burthensome to his mind, that he has no room to think of the mouse and the wren, the emmet and the mite, the green myriads of the peopled grass, the many-tribed weeds of the field, or the dancing motes that glitter in the noontide beams?

Since then we know of no boundaries to circumscribe the divine Omniscience, but that it may extend to every thing without overlooking any thing, and discern remotest consequences in their present causes, why should we scruple to admit that he gave being to those causes with a view to their

their confequences? and on the formation of a world difpofed his fubftances, material and fpiritual, with fuch properties, powers, fituations, motions and ideas, as fhould produce the exact feries of events he intended to bring forth?

In this cafe there is no occafion nor room for controuling or altering the operation of fecond caufes, they being already adjufted to anfwer all the purpofes they were deftined to compleat. And if there be fupernatural interpofitions (which I neither affirm nor deny) we cannot fuppofe them made upon unforefeen emergencies to fupply defects in the original contrivance, but comprized therein, as being judged proper for manifeftation of the divine power and government to intelligent creatures, and worked up into one uniform plan, together with the operations of fecondary agents.

§. 46. In this view of the œconomy of Providence, we fee that any abfolute decree or fecret fatality to enforce the execution of a defign againft the tendency of fecond second causes to turn it aside, must be superfluous, provision being already made in perfect wisdom for every event which is to take effect by disposition of the causes proper to give it birth, nor will any of those causes deviate into another tendency than that they were calculated to take.

Thus it appears, that all things fall out according to the will and disposition of God, and conformably to the scheme of his Providence, working for the most part, if not always by the ministry of material or voluntary agents: but the methods whereby this ministry is conducted are various. Some parts of the plan are accomplished by the choice and industry of man, instigated thereto by appetites, judgements, imaginations, desires, obligations, dangers, and other motives; other parts are executed by the stated laws of nature, such as the instinct[a] of brutes, action of the ele-

---

[a] Which, we have seen in a former note, is something between necessary and free Agency; but in general estimation, seems ranked under the former. And what we do ourselves without reflection, or consciousness, is commonly stiled mechanical.

ments, powers of vegetation, qualities of soils, changes of seasons, and vicissitudes of night and day; and others brought about by the courses of fortune dependant upon the situations ᵇ of substances, and their mutual applications upon one another, to us accidental and uninvestigable.

But what proceeds from the two first of these causes, we do not usually ascribe to the hand of Fate: for nobody looks upon it as a Fatality that last winter is now succeeded by summer; that the days are long, the air warm, the corn and fruits begin to ripen, for all these are natural, nor could any body expect things should have fallen out otherwise. So neither do we think a parent fated to put his son out to school,

---

ᵇ The powers of second causes belong to Nature; but their concurrence, or coming to where they may operate, lies within the province of Fortune. That flame should burn wood is nothing strange: but that the candle should be left close to the wainscot was unlucky. So we know well enough there are causes in nature capable of raising a storm: but that they should be ready at hand to raise it with violence, and drive it upon our forests, or our houses, makes the misfortune.

for

for it was his defire to give him a good education, and his choice and judgement directed him to the proper methods for effecting it.

Therefore the laſt claſs of cauſes only remains for the province of Fate, to wit, ſuch whoſe operations are fortuitous and unaccountable, that is, beyond the reach of human foreſight and ſagacity to diſcover; neverthelefs they muſt have ſome certain ſprings and iſſues, as well as the motions of nature or actions of men.

§. 47. Thus the ſame events lie under the difpoſal of Fate and of Fortune, and both terms take their riſe from our manner of conceiving things. Chance is no agent nor power, but the creature only of imagination, deriving its birth from our ignorance; for when we ſee cauſes at work, but know not their tendency, we ſay it is a chance what they will produce: therefore that which is chance to one man may be none to another, who has better information

tion or more judgement to difcern the train things are taking.

If a die were to be thrown, the caft would be produced by the motions of the thrower's arm, the fhape of the box, inequalities of the table, and other imperceptible circumftances, of which we can make no eftimate, therefore we deem it to lie under the power of Chance; but were the caft to determine between two malefactors which of them fhould fuffer, we fhould then think it a matter worthy referring to the fupreme difpofer of all events, for the lot cometh from the Lord; yet ftill being uncertain what means he will employ, or what effect they fhall take, we attribute the decifion to his Will or Decree, fkipping over that undifcernible chain of caufes lying between his firft appointment and thofe now in act.

Therefore Fate and Fortune feem for the moft part to claim a concurrent jurifdiction, many tracts lying within the province of both: and under this apprehenfion we exprefs ourfelves upon common occafions;

for

for when we hear of a man falling in battle, we say indifferently, it was his Fate, or his Fortune to be slain; and of a young person intended to be sent abroad, but uncertain in what business, or what place he may find opportunities for settling, we say, it is doubtful where his lot may fall, where fortune may carry him, or his fate or destiny fix him.

But to which of these powers we shall ascribe the influence, depends upon the objects we take into contemplation: while we regard only the secret springs and unforeseen incidents which may affect an event, we deem it in the hand of Fortune: but when we look on further to that intelligent Being, who is the disposer of all events, we conceive that those springs will work, and incidents fall out, according to his direction and decree.

Nevertheless it is obvious, as we observed before, that a decree will work nothing without an application of power to enforce the execution of it, and when such application has been made by provision

of

of the proper means for bringing an event to pass, a decree or declaration of the purpose intended becomes needless: for the requisite measures being once taken, will have their effect, whether any word be spoken concerning them or no. Therefore the issues of things proceed, and fortune derives her efficacy, from the provision not the decree of the Almighty, from the work of his hand, not the word of his mouth; and this latter, if any such there were, added nothing to the acts of Omnipotence, but must be delivered for some other purpose than to ensure the completion of his design.

§. 48. Hence it appears, that in using the terms Fate, Decree or Destiny, we speak after the manner of men; for it being customary with us, whenever we resolve upon some distant work, to declare our intentions to persons under our influence, who may assist in compleating it, and to fix a determination in our minds which may render us vigorous, and keep us watchful

Fate.

in the profecution, we conceive of God as making the like declared or mental determination with regard to every fpot he comprifes within the plan of his Providence.

Then again, being fenfible this determination cannot operate upon the courfes of fortune as a command, yet that fomething muft operate to put them in motion, and being unable to trace, or even to conceive a chain of caufes extending from the firft formation of the plan to all thefe multifarious events, we cannot help acknowledging muft come to pafs by the divine appointment, we get an obfcure idea of an irrefiftible force, a fomething we cannot explain nor account for its exiftence, which we call a Fatality, which perpetually hangs over fecond caufes, conftraining their motions, or like an adamantine wall, confining them within their appointed courfe, from whence they would have a natural propenfity to deviate. Thus Fatality becomes disjoined from the decree, and lofes the proper import belonging to it by its derivation, being now no longer a *fatum*

or

or word spoken, but one knows not well what; an emanation from it, like light from the sun-beams, a power without an agent to exert it; for when God has spoken, his action ceases, and the Fatality is a consequence of what he has said.

That this is the sense, if a sense it may be called, that men ordinarily affix to the term, appears by the Atheists employing it, who acknowledge no intelligent Being who might *fari*, that is, speak or issue a decree: for being called upon to assign a cause for the laws and establishments of nature, they ascribed them to a blind Fatality, working upon the mass of matter throughout the universe, and driving it into a regular form. But if we regard etymology, a blind fatality is as absurd an expression as that of a dumb decree, or an unintended design. The *Epicureans* alone discarded Fate upon a most unphilosophical principle, that events may ensue, such as the declination of atoms, without any prior cause whatever to produce them: but all who admitted an eternal First Cause, whether in-

telligent

Fate.

telligent or unsentient, seem to have entertained a notion of Fatality.

This confused and indeterminate notion opened the door to judicial Astrology[a], for though the stars were supposed by their positions to affect the lives of men, I never yet heard it attempted to be shown in what manner, or by what mediums they operated: but a conformity being once fancied between the successes of human transactions and aspects of the heavenly bodies, it was a short way to talk of a Fatality, though nobody could tell why, or how, or by what channels the connection should be effected.

The like may be said of the *Parcæ*, whose singing answers to the decree utter-

---

[a] And to the Art Magic, and Prognostications by dreams, omens, prodigies, prickings into the bible, strangers in the candle, screechings of owls, influences of a rainy *Friday* upon the following week, and other the like trumpery, maintained by the Stoics in *Tully*'s Divination, and by our modern old women in the nursery. For all these are not esteemed as Revelations, but as a consent or sympathy in things, between which the Philosopher and Naturalist cannot find the least connection.

ed, and could have no other effect than to amuse themselves and lighten their task; but it was the thread they spun which determined the duration and colour of men's lives beyond the power of *Jove* himself to alter: yet we never hear of their having any communication with sublunary affairs, or acting as efficient causes upon any thing moving here; nevertheless upon their spinning, there instantly arose a sympathetic energy in the causes at work upon earth, drawing them to produce an issue conformable to what was spun.

§. 49. We see from the foregoing observations, how the term Fate has slid off its original basis, being departed from its first signification, that of a decree or resolve of the Almighty to a something generated thereby, an undefinable influence, residing neither in body, nor soul, nor substance, but an abstract force or activity [a], hovering

---

[a] Which there is no agent to exert. Not God, for his action was compleated long ago, upon issuing the decree: nor second causes, for they are supposed to be turned aside from their natural operation by the Fatality.

as it were in the air, and operating upon the caufes of things as they feverally begin to act.

Nor yet do men keep always fteady to this idea of Fate in their common converfation; for we often hear them talk of the Fate of a convict criminal lying in the hand of the Prince who has power to pardon or to order execution; the lover waits for the decifion of his miftrefs to fix his Fate; the poet talks of phyficians iffuing mandates in arreft of Fate [b], and an unexpected accident or arrival of a timely fuccour is thought fometimes to change the Fate of a battle: whereas if we regard the genuine notion of Fate, it was fixed long ago by the decree of heaven; nor is it in the power of man, or any natural agent, to determine or ftop, or change, or affect it in any refpect.

[b] *With looks demure they grafp the golden bait,*
And iffue mandates in arreft of fate.
THURSTON.

Who being a lawyer, took his metaphor from the law courts, arrefting or ftopping judgement after a verdict for irregularities fhown in the proceedings.

These variations of language do not disturb us in our ordinary discourses, for the context or occasion introducing them moulds our words into the shape that is proper; but men of thought and abstraction, desirous of affixing constantly the same ideas to their words, find themselves disappointed when they light upon a term of vague and unstable signification; for as we generally think in words, and their sense in the various phrases whereto we join them, is determined by custom; we are led insensibly in the progress of our reasonings to understand them differently, from whence great confusion and perplexity must unavoidably ensue.

Therefore the science of language, and exact observation of ideas adhering thereto, would help us greatly in our discoveries of nature; for if men could fix upon terms not liable to variation of sense or misapprehension, their disputes would be shortened, and they might quickly arrive at so much knowledge as is attainable by human understanding. We have found no reason

reason hitherto to disregard the admonitions of our present patroness Philology, they having been helpful to us upon several occasions; and she informs us, the word Fate carries a very loose and indeterminate signification.

For this reason I wish it were quite expunged from the philosophical vocabulary, and Providence substituted in its room, which I conceive would render our thoughts clearer and less intricate, and give them a freer progress when turned upon the government of the world; for the provisions of heaven in the original disposition of adequate causes may answer all purposes, as well those accomplished by natural as accidental means, or the motions of free agency.

§. 50. But men find a difficulty in conceiving of absolute dominion, without a coercive authority or compulsion exercised upon the subjects under it: which makes us all so fond of power as a necessary means for bringing our purposes to bear against the opposition of other agents which might attempt to defeat them. Yet in many inſtances, as has been remarked in §. 19. we ourſelves can make proviſion for deſigns wherein other perſons are to concur, and guide their conduct ſo far as we know what will move them, and have the proper motives in our hands, without pretending to any authority or compulſive power over them. And if there be always ſome hazard of a diſappointment, it is becauſe we can never ſee thoroughly the exact ſtate of their deſires, nor what external accidents, ſuch as weather, diſeaſe, or the like, may diſturb the ſucceſs of our ſchemes: but were there nothing extraneous to interfere, and had we a perfect knowledge of men's minds, much more, were their inclinations and judgements of our framing, we ſhould need no deſpotic juriſdiction nor controuling power to guide them into what courſes of behaviour we pleaſed.

Now there is nothing external to the work of God. The laws of nature bringing forth her various productions were of

his

his establishment: the workings of chance followed from some determinate causes, though to us unknown; these again from other prior, and so on in a continual channel from the sources first opened by the exertion of his power; for no event, however casual, can happen without something occasioning it to fall out in that manner: the actions of men proceed according to their apprehensions and judgements thrown upon them by their constitution or temperament, by education, by company and occurrences befalling them in life; all which were conveyed by nature or fortune, and therefore must be referred to the origin from whence they derived. For every effect must be produced by the action of some agent material or spiritual, or the concurrence of several, and must follow according to the manner of that action being exerted; which manner was determined by some impulse or motive impressed from elsewhere; nor can we stop until we arrive at some act of Omnipotence.

Thus

Thus the face of things, as well in the moral as natural kingdoms, results from the qualities, positions*, and motions God

* The secondary qualities of bodies result from their form, which is nothing else than a certain position of their component parts: for the same shillings laid upon a table, will make a square, a lozenge, a ring, or a cross, according as you place them; and the same particles of matter will make grass, or mutton, or human flesh, according as they are disposed among one another by digestion. The modifications of our organs occasioning them to impress their several perceptions, can be conceived no otherwise than as depending upon their figures or motions: so that though Thought be neither figure nor motion, it follows precisely upon the changes made in either; and this whether we work those changes ourselves, or have them produced before us by other causes.

The secondary qualities of spirit depend upon its position, in some organization; for if the spirit of a man were placed in his great toe, he would neither see nor hear, nor understand; and if it were placed in the organization of an oyster, perhaps he might have no more sense than that stupid animal. Motion serves only to change positions into one another, and what effect it shall have depends upon prior positions: for the same motion of a bullet will destroy this man or that, according to the position of the musket, or places they occupy: and the same particles of beef are capable, or not, of being moved about by the circulation for our nourishment, according to their internal position in the joint when it is raw or roasted, or putrefied.

gave

gave to his substances at the formation of a world. It remains only, that we ask ourselves the question, whether he extended his plan to a compass larger than he could comprehend himself, or gave birth to causes which might produce events unthought of by him, or more numerous than he could grasp in his Omniscience? If we answer in the negative, we must needs acknowledge that provision was made at the beginning for all that train of events, and accomplishment of those purposes we have seen, or shall hereafter see effected.

But experience testifies, that this provision leaves many things in our power, and circumscribes us in many other respects; we lay schemes, and take measures appearing certain to succeed, but find them fail in the issue, and that by accidents we could not have expected, nor can account for their happening; our reason deserts us in time of need; we commit blunders, and give into follies we could not have thought ourselves capable of: tempests, earthquakes, famines, pestilences, and destructive diseases cases arise from no natural causes that we can discern; and our experience of those things gives us the notion of Fatality. Therefore Fate, if we will needs employ the term in our speculations, is that part of the divine provision producing events which would not have ensued by the known laws of nature, nor operation of observable causes, nor contrivances of man, but are rather contrary to his endeavours.

§. 51. *Seneca*, in *Nat. Quæst.* Lib. II. cap. 36. defines Fate the necessity of all things and actions, which no force can break through: and he seems herein to have given Fate the import belonging to it in common propriety of language; for the courses of Fate are always deemed irresistible and unalterable; nor do we apply the term unless to cases wherein the will and power of man has no concern.

Therefore when a person fails in a distemper, we say it was his Fate to die, because we suppose his wish and endeavours were bent upon preventing it: but if he escapes,

escapes, we do not say he was fated to recover, but at most that his Fate was not yet come, that is, has not yet operated upon him; for this was the effect of the cares taken to save him.

If we happen to ruin a scheme we were extremely fond of accomplishing through some palpable misconduct of our own, we think ourselves under a fatal infatuation, because every body is conceived willing to employ his best judgement for his own benefit; from whence comes the observation, that whom *Jove* would destroy, he first deprives of their understanding: but if we chance to succeed beyond expectation by a more than ordinary dexterity of management, we think nothing of a Fatality, because the unusual clearness of judgement and success consequent thereupon, were things agreeable to our wish, and effects of bestirring ourselves in the exercise of our faculties.

So likewise a fatal accident is that which brings on an event, we are extremely averse to: whereas a lucky incident is never termed fatal,

fatal, becaufe tending to further our advancement towards fomething we defire.

But if *Seneca* was right in calling Fate a Neceffity, which no force can break thro', we cannot think him fo in the extent he has given to its dominion, comprehending all things and all actions: for this fwallows up the whole province of Freewill, to which Fate and Neceffity, in every body's underftanding, are counted diametrically oppofite: for what is fated to happen does not lie in my power to prevent, and what depends upon my pleafure and option, is yet undetermined by any Fatality.

Nor let it be thought we injure him, by taking his expreffion too ftrictly; for he goes on, in cap. 38. to particularize in matters belonging directly to human management. If, fays he, it be fated that fuch a young perfon fhall become eloquent, it is likewife fated that he fhall ftudy rhetoric; if that he fhall grow rich, it is fated that he fhall trade to foreign parts. In like manner his brother Stoic, *Chryfippus*, infifts, in *Tully de Fato*, cap. 13. that when a sick man is fated to recover, it is confated that he shall send for a physician; to which it might be added, and that the doctor shall use his best skill, and the apothecary dispense his recipes properly.

But any common eye may see, that these Fates do not carry such a necessity as the force of man cannot break through: for the scholar, if he pleases, may neglect his studies, the young trader squander away his stock in extravagancies and debaucheries, the sick person persist obstinately in refusing help, the doctor destroy his patient, or the apothecary impose upon both by neglecting to provide good drugs, or mixing up ingredients that will do mischief.

What then! are not eloquence, riches, and health, the blessings of heaven? are they not given to those whom God thinks proper, and withheld from whom he pleases? Or can any, to whom he designs a favour, ever fail of receiving the effects of his bounty? By no means; nor does this consequence follow from our rejection of

Fatality;

Fatality: for tho' all things are not fated, yet all things are wisely provided, so as to take the train requisite for compleating whatever events were contained within his plan. Thus the orator and merchant were provided by education, example, and other natural means, with a disposition for improving the talents and opportunities put into their hands; the sick man is provided with sense to know the value of life, and fondness for its preservation; the medical assistants with compassion to a fellow-creature in distress, with skill and diligence and a desire to maintain their credit in their professions: and these dispositions will infallibly put them upon taking those measures voluntarily, which they had full power and free liberty to have omitted.

Thus the will of God is done without employing the compulsive force of Fate, or rigid arm of Necessity. But the difficulties that have always perplexed the speculative upon this subject, spring from their not observing the double sense of the word *possible*, as it relates to power or to contingency, remarked

in

in the foregoing pages, §. 30, 31; for want of which they could not conceive how any thing could be left to the power and option of man, without inferring a poffibility that he might defeat the purpofes of God: but having well fettled that diftinction in our minds, and taking along with us that the behaviour of men follows upon their apprehenfions and fentiments which refult from the feen and unfeen fprings employed by God in his adminiftration of the moral world, we may eafily comprehend how it may be poffible, that is, in the power of man, in many inftances to fruftrate his defigns; neverthelefs he may fo perfectly know what will be the defires and thoughts of their hearts, that there is no poffibility, that is, no danger, they fhould purfue any other than the particular tenour of conduct moft conducive thereto.

§. 52. The effence of Fate lying in its unchangeablenefs and independence on the turns of Freewill, the powers of different perfons being various, and coming or going according as opportunity changes, there is no paradox in afferting, that the fame event may be under the arbitrary difpofal of one man, which is fated and neceffary to another, and may be matter of choice to-day, which was efteemed the work of Fate yefterday, and may be fo again to-morrow.

Suppofe you and I could give evidence againſt fomebody of a capital offence unknown to any body elfe; but there being fome favourable circumftances in his cafe, we went into a room together to confult whether we fhould make the difcovery or no: this we fhould be apt to call fitting to fix his Fate; and any body upon feeing us come out, and knowing what we had been about, might properly afk, well, what is his Fate? is he doomed to die? But though our decifion be reckoned Fate, with refpect to the culprit, as being unalterable and inevitable by him, yet we fhould not efteem ourfelves under a Fatality or Neceffity to profecute, becaufe it would ftill remain in our power to do it or forbear.

Marriages

Fate.

Marriages are commonly faid to be made in heaven; yet it is of the very effence of marriage to have the free confent of the parties; for the folemnization follows upon their will and defire; but the caufes influencing their choice were not of their own procurement, but extraneous and fortuitous to them. A man determined to fettle in the world, but unprovided of his object, may think it in the hand of Fate or Fortune what qualified party he fhall meet with; but when the acquaintance is made, the liking fixed, and matters agreed on both fides, things proceed thence forward under the direction of Choice and Freewill: then again, if afterwards fhe prove a fhrew, he may chance to curfe his ftars for fubjecting him to fo cruel a Fate.

The fall of *Troy* was faid to be written in the book of Fate before its foundation; yet the parties inftrumental thereto, *Paris* and *Helen*, the *Grecian* Princes, the council of *Priam* refufing reftitution, acted by paffion, contrivance, defign, and deliberation, thofe fprings of free agency: and

during

during the siege, the poor *Trojans* used their utmost efforts to ward off the stroke of Fate, which nevertheless fell inevitably upon them.

Thus when Fate has begun his course, it opens at intervals to let in Freewill, who having played her part, the stream closes again, and involves all before it in irresistible necessity.

From hence it appears, that in disquisitions upon this subject our business is to enquire not so much into the nature of things, as the import of expressions and state of ideas under contemplation; and we shall often find that the same event, according to the persons concerned in it, to the light wherein we place it, or to our considering the whole or some part only of the chain whereon it hangs, shall be either the work of Fate, the effect of Chance, or the product of human Industry, Forethought and Option. For Fate and Necessity being always opposed to free Choice, may be applicable to an Event or

not,

not, according to whose choice, or what act of the will you refer it.

If I lie under the power of a superiour in what manner to dispose of me, the determination is Fate to me, though matter of choice and deliberation to him. So I may esteem it in the hand of Fate to determine how I shall dispose of myself seven years hence, if I cannot by any present act of mine certainly direct my future resolves; but when the time of action comes, I shall then have it my power and option which way to turn myself: then again, after I have executed my choice and fixed my situation, if I run back through the whole chain of causes bringing me thereinto, the opportunities enabling, and inducements prevailing on me to take the part I did, which were not of my own procurement, I may be apt to call it the work of Fate.

No wonder then that so variable and slippery a term should often present us with double lights, bewildering the most cautious traveller, like an *ignis fatuus*: wherefore, as I said before, it were better we could

could do entirely without it; for Providence seems a much clearer and steadier idea; nor are there the like difficulties in understanding how that, by the apt disposition of causes suited to each respective purpose, may generate the laws of nature, shape the windings of fortune, and produce the motives giving the turn to human volition.

§. 53. Let us now consider how far our conduct and condition in life may be cramped and controuled by this universal provision. We find ourselves circumscribed in our powers, our knowledge, and the scope allotted us to exercise them. This nobody doubts. The severities of winter succeed the conveniencies of summer; our weight binds us down to the earth, nor can we soar aloft like the swallow. Tempests, diseases, and sinister accidents come upon us inevitably, and many things fall out beyond our skill or power to prevent them: but want of skill and power is not want of liberty. Bars, obstructions,

and

and restraints confine us in the exercise of those powers we have; but there is a difference between freedom of action and freedom of will: the latter respects only such things as we have a natural ability to perform, and against which there lies no impediment to prevent the success of our endeavours. But Freewill cannot proceed without inducements to move, and ideas to direct it; therefore that provision which supplies us with these, is so far from overthrowing, that it is the basis and support of our freedom.

Nor would doubts arise concerning our possession of this privilege, if we did not generally extend it beyond its proper object, which, strictly speaking, is no other than the present action in our power; but our present endeavours often have a tendency to distant purposes; and experience teaches us what they have been used to produce; therefore we esteem the consequences to be effected by them as under our power, and subjects of our option: then, if such remote events fall out otherwise than expected, we ascribe it to a Fatality; whereas the failure was really owing to particular circumstances we did not attend to, or the interfering of natural causes we did not take into account.

More especially we conceive ourselves masters of our own ideas, and to have the constant use of that judgement and discretion we possess; therefore if they fail us at any time in some egregious misconduct, we apprehend ourselves as having been under a secret infatuation; because the proceeding being contrary to our present and former will and judgement, which we can scarce believe could have varied so greatly in the interval, we conclude a force must have been put upon our Will to make it act so opposite to its own designs.

But it is well known, that our apprehensions are not always the same, nor does reason always operate with equal vigour; imagination varies her scenes, discretion falls off her guard, fancies start up, desires intrude, passions beguile, and things present themselves in unusual aspects, owing

Fate.

to the state of our bodily humours, the mechanical play of our organization, prevalency of our habits, and appearance of external objects; all which are natural causes acting with a regularity undiscernible to ourselves. So there is no occasion for recurring to that unsubstantial Fatality spoken of in §. 48. for Fate is so much of the order of second causes, as our Will has no share in carrying on, and our Understanding no light to discover.

Thus Fate and Freewill have their distinct provinces, nor ever appear to clash unless when we happen to mistake the boundaries; but if we esteem events within our power which depend upon other causes, we may find ourselves frustrated, not by a force upon our will, but by having undertaken more, and carried our expectations further than we were warranted. For the giant Fate, though enormous in strength and stature, never tramples upon Liberty, nor so covers the ground as not to leave some space for human Agency while employed in its proper offices.

§. 54. For

§. 54. For we have nothing to do with Events lying within the bosom of Fate, nor are we to take our measures upon any thing we may fancy contained there: it may affect the success, but cannot alter the prudence of our conduct, which consists in the conformity of our actions with the best lights of our judgement.

If God has any secret purpose to accomplish, no doubt he has provided causes to work it out; our business lies only with those causes whose existence and tendency we can discern; while we make the due use of them, so far as we have power and opportunity, we shall perform our little share in the execution of his plan.

When we have determined upon our point ever so wisely, and projected our scheme ever so prudently, perhaps there may be a decree to a contrary effect which will baffle all our endeavours; but this can be no guide to us, nor object of our contemplation, until manifesting itself by the completion: in the mean time, if we find

things

Fate.

things take a wrong turn unexpectedly, we are not from thence to infer there is a Fatality [a] upon them, for we cannot expect to penetrate into the secret workings of Fate, which are purposely concealed from us, but must employ our skill and industry to rectify our measures, while there remains any probability of success, that is, until we perceive invincible obstacles standing apparently in the way.

Nor have we the less range of action for the secret springs of events taking their certain course by the divine appointment,

---

[a] Yet if we have often tried the same scheme unsuccessfully, this is a reason why we should desist from attempting it any more: not as convinced of a Fatality, but of a defectiveness in the scheme, or of there being some natural obstacles which we do not perceive. For the frequency of an event is an evidence in multitudes of cases, of there being adequate causes to produce it again, though we may not investigate them. Thus if a farmer has several times planted a field with barley, but never could find a crop at harvest, he will do wisely to sow no more there; being persuaded there is something either in the soil, or situation, unfit for that grain, though he discerns no apparent difference of either from other grounds. This observation would be very useful for projectors, who persist obstinately in supporting theory against experience.

neither

neither would our liberty be at all enlarged, if they were set in motion by the fortuitous declination of *Epicurus*'s atoms. Experience teaches that our strongest expectations are liable to be frustrated, and our best projected schemes rendered abortive unaccountably; and we should stand equally at a loss how to ward off the disappointment whether it were to come by chance or by Fate, for we can as little conjecture what the wild workings of chance would produce, as the stated provisions of wisdom: in both cases we can only proceed according to what we see, and put in use those methods which we judge most expedient. Nor would it prove less destructive of care and industry, if we should entertain a notion of luck [b] running against us, than of a Fatality.

Predestination.

§. 55. There is one species of Fate respecting the condition of each man in ano-

---

[b] Prevailing much among gamesters, sometimes doing them great detriment; and which by an easy transition they often turn into Fatality.

ther life dependant on his conduct in this, commonly called Predestination. This, in many people's apprehension, carries with it the idea of a Fatality; for they say the Saint cannot sin, nor the Sinner do right: yet it being obvious there can be neither right nor wrong, unless in things within our power and option, they suppose that though we have power to perform, we have none to choose, so there lies a force upon the will constraining it to one particular choice.

But experience does not support this doctrine, for the wicked now and then use their power well, and it is too notorious that the righteous often fail of doing the good they might. Did *Peter* act right when he thrice denied his master? Or did *Pilate* act wrong in using endeavours to get *Jesus* released instead of *Barabbas*? and does not this manifest, that neither were under a constant fatality, but left sometimes at least at liberty to depart from their general tenour of conduct?

Then

Then if any pretend that this general tenour, so far as requisite to denominate the party good or bad, is influenced by the fatality of a decree; let them search into the recesses of the human heart, examine the judgements, desires, imaginations harbouring there, understand perfectly all the natural causes anywise affecting them, and clearly discern that none of these are adequate to the effect, before they are warranted to assert this. Nor let them build too hastily upon the dictates of authority, which are best explained by experience of facts, and are delivered in a language accommodated to the common conceptions of men, wherein we often ascribe events to the act of God, which were the result of second causes established by him.

Therefore it may be true that God giveth us both to will and to do, without constraining our Wills by his immediate and irresistible influence; as it is true, that he giveth us our daily bread, though he sends it not by special messengers, as he did to *Elias*, but by the provisions he made for the

Predestination.

the fruits of nature in the structure of plants, fertility of soils, kindly warmth of the sun, seasonable refreshments of dews and showers, and by the provisions he made for exerting human industry, and fixing an attachment to their several professions in the farmer, the miller, the mealman, and the baker [a].

§. 56. It must be acknowledged that the final state of every man, as well as all other events without exception, depends upon causes flowing from springs originally provided by the Almighty; and in this light it may be said that none shall be saved whose names were not written in the book of life [b]: but the writing in this book, if we

[a] So are our schools, our universities, our treatises of divinity and morality, our histories, our encouragements for learning and industry, our establishments of divine services and sermons, so many provisions made for giving us to will: and though now and then they may give us to will what we had better have let alone, yet we should find great miss if we were totally deprived of them.

[b] And the like may be said with regard to other events as well as our future state. For none shall be a scholar,

Predestination.

we will employ the figure, has no efficacy, nor can limit our freedom, being no more than a declaration or record of the caufes in act, and operations of under-caufes flowing from them; which are equally matter of record, whether running in the channel of freewill, or of impulfe, force, and neceffity.

And the provifions now fpoken of encroach leaft of any upon the province of free Agency; a man may have his bones broken, his fortune ruined, his life deftroyed, by earthquakes, tempefts, plagues, or other accidents he cannot poffibly guard againft nor prevent; but his interefts in futurity cannot be hurt, unlefs by fome action he has power and liberty to forbear. Therefore is he free in whatever he does affecting thofe interefts, notwithftanding

fcholar, a foldier, a merchant, a poftillion, or a chimney-fweeper; none fhall get to the *Eaft* or *Weft Indies*, nor fhall build a houfe, or lay out a garden, whofe names are not written in the book, as deftined to thofe purpofes: that is, for whom caufes were not provided, enabling and leading them to the accomplifhment.

the entry recorded, or provision preordained; for liberty, as we have seen before, depends upon the act ensuing the exertion of our power, not upon any thing antecedent, nor upon the motives or causes inciting us to exert it: if we have talents, opportunities, understanding and discretion, we have the same freedom to use them by what means soever they came to us, whether by a sudden and accidental good fortune, or by a long series of causes preappointed for that purpose.

But men are led by their averseness to trouble to extend the idea of their power beyond its proper bounds, they want to do something to-day whereby to ensure an indefeasible title to future happiness, without leaving any thing for to-morrow, but to take their pastime in the manner most agreeable to themselves. This is mistaking their province, for they can never do their work so compleatly but there will always remain something further to do: yet this does not affect their liberty to take such measures as at present are feasible, for whatever be predestined concerning them, to-morrow they may still do so much for themselves as the actions now in their power amount to.

Therefore it behoves us to stand always upon the watch, to observe every succeeding moment what comes into our power, and to employ it so as may turn most for our benefit: for Predestination rightly understood, operates by our hands, and the course we steer is always that it takes upon every particular occasion, unless when it employs external causes not under our controul, and these we have no business with; where indeed we could know the success depends solely upon such causes [b], our cares and

---

[b] For our future conduct may be determined by them: we can only make our resolves properly, but whether they shall remain in full colour and vigour depends in great measure upon the temperament of our bodies, the company we fall into, or temptations assailing us: so much of these, as we cannot foresee nor provide against, it would be fruitless to solicit ourselves about, nor have we any thing else to do with respect to them, than confide in that Providence which orders all things for the best. But so far as we can help ourselves

Predestination.

and endeavours were superfluous, but in matters depending upon ourselves, our opinion or disbelief of their being predestined in the manner above described by a provision of the proper causes for enabling, moving, and directing us, how to bestir ourselves, makes no alteration in the rule of our conduct. For if a merchant breeds up his son to industry, instructs him in the misteries of trade, and furnishes him a competent stock, with a certain foreknowledge and determination that he shall make a fortune thereby: neverthelefs the same diligence, the same circumspection, and the same methods of proceeding will be requisite as if those advantages had fallen upon him accidentally, and the success been absolutely unknown to every body.

§. 57. But it is not enough to take off the discouragements against deliberation

ourselves by any present act, either to prevent them, or prepare our minds against them, we may use the powers and opportunities put into our hands with the same freedom, whether we conceive them derived to us by a preappointment, or otherwise.

and activity, unless we quiet the apprehensions arising in men's minds concerning their future proceedings: for some disturb themselves with the dread of a predetermination upon all their motions, which may turn them hereafter into the road of destruction, notwithstanding the best dispositions they find at present in their hearts. But let them consider, that their present actions were as much predestined as any they shall perform hereafter, yet they find themselves at full liberty to shape them in such manner as they judge expedient; therefore they may depend upon having the like freedom at other times.

Well, but they know not what ideas may then start up in their minds urging them to misapply their powers. Is there not the like hazard attending the common affairs of life? for other events, as well as those affecting the moral character, are equally predestined by the provision of causes suited to bring them forth. Yet who that lives in peace and plenty ever affrights himself with the thought that there

there may be secret springs at work which may deprive him of his health, his limbs, or his substance^a? While things go on in a good train, and no danger discernible to human circumspection threatens, we rest contented with our situation, unmolested by imaginary terrors, and so we may with respect to our spiritual concerns, for virtue improves itself, and good habits grow stronger by exercise: therefore though our

---

[a] Yet there are those who in the midst of affluence affright themselves with the apprehension that they shall want: but this is always looked upon as the effect of distemper: and so are the like terrors of any other kind. Few labour under more than one sort of these disturbances: he that fancies infections in the air does not think of wanting; and he that dreads the approach of want, is not sollicitous about his future state. Therefore let each make himself consistent throughout, and learn from his easiness under the bare possibility of one mischief, to take courage against the like possibility of another. Nor may there want room for honest artifice in curing distempers of this sort: an alarm raised of rogues or fire would probably suspend any doubts of the religious kind. For it is not unnatural that one terror should banish another. I believe the old women upon the banks of the *Weser* or the *Fulda* (if there be any still left unstarved) have something else to think on than Election and Reprobation.

final state remains in the hand of Providence, and we cannot penetrate the secret councils of heaven, yet the right dispositions we feel at present, are an evidence that provision is made for a happy issue at last, an evidence sufficient to exclude every thing more than a possibility of our failing: nor were it expedient that this should be excluded, as being serviceable to keep us vigilant, and guard us against a supineness of temper that might creep upon us insensibly.

Besides, let us examine wherein it would better our condition, if God were to revoke his Predestination, and undo his provision of causes, so far as relates to ourselves : would this enable us by our present cares so to bind our future conduct as that it could never run amiss? and if not, how would matters be mended with us? There would still remain a possibility that after having begun well we might faint in the midway, and this event would become absolutely fortuitous: but we should hardly find more comfort in thinking that our Fate

Fate depended upon the caſt of a die than upon a Predetermination.

So then it might fairly be put to men's choice whether they had rather believe themſelves in the hand of Chance, or of a wiſe and gracious Governour: for the proceedings of wiſdom are regular, and tho' we know not perfectly what belongs to goodneſs, we may form a judgement thereon ſatisfactory to any reaſonable perſon; but the flighty gambols of chance are objects of no ſcience, nor grounds of any dependance whatever.

Nor ſhould we find greater ſecurity in the privilege of indifference ſo much vaunted by ſome, for this being controulable by no motives, it would avail us little to have a ſober underſtanding and virtuous inclinations moving us to take a ſalutary courſe; for our Freewill of indifference might run counter to them all, nor could we have any aſſurance what turns it might take: which muſt throw us again into all the anxieties attendant upon the dominion of chance.

Thus whatever hypothesis we can frame, leaves as much room for apprehensions as that of Predestination above described, for while we conceive it operating not by a Fatality, but by an apt disposition of second causes, it gives as large a scope to human freedom and forecast, and industry, as we have reason from experience to think ourselves possessed of, and as good ground of expectation from the success of our measures as we are warranted in any light to entertain.

§. 58. Nevertheless, if the mind appears to have taken a wrong turn, are there not just grounds of apprehension? Most assuredly. But this turn manifests itself most evidently in the prevalence of evil habits, and attachment to present pleasures, without regard to the consequences; therefore those who stand in greatest danger, are least apt to take the alarm, and whoever could raise it in them, would do them an inestimable kindness. On the contrary, such in whom disquietudes abound, have upon

upon that very account the less reason to entertain them; for an earnest concern for the future being the first and principal spring provided for bringing men into the right way, where this appears strongly, it is of itself alone an evidence that provision has been made in their favour.

But despondencies of this kind are often owing to the indiscretion of teachers, who insist too strenuously upon higher perfections of virtue than human nature can attain, and are found to prevail most upon women, or persons of small ability, and in their contemplative hours rather than seasons of action. For the consolation of such persons therefore let it be observed, that righteousness does not consist in the quantity of good we do, but in our doing so much, be it little, or be it much, as lies in our power. There are pegs and pins in a building as well as beams and columns, nor can we doubt that God distributes to every man the talents suited to the task he is to perform; therefore if we attend only to family affairs, or making broths

broths for the sick, provided this be all we had ability to do, we have compleated our part.

Let it next be remarked, that our imagination does not lie under our absolute command to raise ideas there, in what strength and vividness of colour we please: the Poet cannot always fill himself with inspiration, nor the Philosopher with his clear discernment of abstracted truth, nor the religious man with his ardors and transports: therefore the want of a fervent faith [a] and glowing zeal is not so much the mark of reprobation, as of a present indisposition of the organs.

Let

---

[a] If any man shall disquiet himself for that he can never rise at all to this fervent faith, let him consider that the capacity of entertaining a strong persuasion, is one of the talents given for carrying us through good works, and God distributes it to men in proportion to the tasks they have to perform. To those whom he calls to persecution, or arduous trials, he will afford a larger measure; but let such as have little to do, content themselves with what suffices for their purpose. Strength of mind is no otherwise in our power than ability of body: we may improve either by exercise, or management, but can never extend them beyond the

Predestination.

Let it further be remembered, that notwithstanding what may have been inculcated of a constant attention to the duties of religion, our business lies chiefly in action, and the common duties of life: so that when perplexities overcloud us, instead of foreboding melancholy omens from the gloom they cast, we should rather take them as admonitions, that it is not now the season to puzzle our brains with thinking, but to bestir ourselves in some active employment, or pursue some innocent recreation, which may supply us with a flow

---

the bounds our natural constitution has prescribed to us. Our common labourers acquire a much greater robustness than others of the same make, brought up to an indolent or sedentary life; but no assiduity in labour can bring a slender loose-built man to toss the weaver's beam of *Goliah*, or carry the gates of *Gaza*. It may be observed further, that our vigour, both of mind and body, grows with our growth, and abates upon our beginning to decay; therefore old women and children, plied injudiciously with good books, are most liable to the disquietudes we have been speaking of. The one may be taught to expect greater lengths than they can yet attain: and the other not to charge it upon themselves as a fault, that they grow feeble and poor in spirit.

of spirits for reason to work with to better purpose afterwards.

For if fear and trembling be a duty, a becoming confidence and just repose in the divine Goodness is a duty likewise, nor is fortitude less a virtue than prudence, and the proper province of both is ascertained by their usefulness[b]. Therefore when anxieties arise, it behoves us to consider what purpose they may answer, while they serve to keep us vigilant, and spur on our activity in helping ourselves, we do well to encourage them; but when they tend to no good, nor urge us to any thing we

---

[b] This shows the benefit of trying our principles of action by their reference to use: for the concern for futurity is one of the moral senses, apt like the others to grow luxuriant, and run into extremes; but what is an extreme can be determined only by examining whether the giving way to it would do more hurt than good. A man is never the nearer heaven for being confident that he shall get there, nor ever the farther from it merely for his apprehensions that he shall not find an entrance. Therefore the former would be the more eligible persuasion, were it not likely to make us remiss and careless in our journey; and the latter is recommendable no further than as it spurs us to activity and vigilance.

should

Predeſtination.

ſhould not have done as well without them, we cannot do better than to turn our face from them, and uſe any expedient at hand to baniſh them out of our thoughts.

But Predeſtination, though formerly making much noiſe in the world, is now grown an unfaſhionable topic [c], nor am I ſorry that it is ſo, for though I think it might be ſo explained as to render it neither formidable nor ſubverſive of diligence, yet I fear ſuch explanation would not ſtick with common apprehenſions, but they would ſtill annex to it an idea of Fatality, which muſt unavoidably nouriſh deſpon-

---

[c] Nor would ever have come into faſhion had it not been for the arts of deſigning perſons, who claim a power of conferring it: for by perſuading mankind that their final happineſs depends upon holding the preciſe form of doctrine taught by themſelves, they inſenſibly infuſe a notion of their having a privilege to admit whom they pleaſe into the number of the Elect, or at leaſt to declare who is one of that number; and impoſe ſuch terms upon the admiſſion as they think moſt for their own advantage. But were Predeſtination really abſolute, no ſubſequent conduct could turn it aſide; nor would it be of more conſequence what a man believes, or whom he follows, than how he lives, or what he practiſes.

dencies

Conclusion.

dencies in phlegmatic tempers, presumption, and fatal security in the sanguine.

Conclusion. §. 59. I have now rummaged every corner of the wilderness, and left no thicket untried that I could think of: it has been my endeavour to open the passages as I went along, and disentangle the boughs where they had matted themselves together, or been interlaced by persons of an unlucky shrewdness in perplexing; so that the traveller may never be drove against the thorns without finding an opening to escape them, nor bewildered in mazes, without feeling a clue to direct him.

Yet I do not pretend so to have cleared the way, as that he may run carelessly along, for the boughs will still overhang, the paths remain dark, rugged, and intricate, and the clue put into his hands be apt to slip away from him; therefore he must not proceed in a hurry, but take every step warily and circumspectly, putting the twigs aside that they may not strike against his eyes, nor intercept his view of

Conclusion.

the ground as he goes along, and keeping good hold of his feveral clues while neceffary for his guidance.

If I have not done my work compleatly to the fatisfaction of every body, allowance may be made for the difficulty of the fubject, which has foiled fo many men of deep thought and learning, that fhould any thing be found here to render it clearer, I fhould rather look upon it as a lucky hit, than any claim to extraordinary merit. For I have not pretended to manage the fame train of argument better than other people, but have proceeded in a method of my own, which if purfued imperfectly, may ftill ferve as a hint, that others may improve upon to greater advantage. I have at leaft to my own content effected a perfect reconcilement between Freewill and Univerfal Providence, and if this could be done to the general content, it would be no fmall fervice to the ferious part of mankind; for neither of thefe points can eafily be given up, nor has it hitherto been found

eafy

easy to show them consistent with one another.

For our reason affords us so many grounds of assurance, that affairs as well in the moral as natural world, are administered by the power and wisdom of God, and yet so many important events, such as the rise and fall of empires, the lives and deaths, the fortunes and distresses of men, depend upon their behaviour among one another, that we cannot but be persuaded he governs the thoughts and actions of mankind with as full and absolute a dominion as he does the courses of nature. On the other hand, daily experience bears witness that our motions lie under our own controul, and we can do this thing or that as we please, without any force constraining, or dominion compelling us to the contrary. Then upon comparing these two considerations together, while they appear to clash, we are tempted to distrust either our reason or our experience; and according to which part we take, either are thrown off our discretion and tenour of conduct by the

Conclusion.

the imagination of a secret influence and compulsion hanging over us, or lose our dependance upon Providence, that truest solace of our minds in time of danger and distress, and surest direction of our conduct in seasons of ease and prosperity.

Whereas were the inconsistency taken off, we might then allow both human agency and divine government their full extent, because they might co-operate in the same work without interfering with each other: we should see no discouragement against making observations upon the things about us relative to our conduct, and taking our measures accordingly with freedom, and a decent confidence in their success, and we should depend contentedly upon the guidance of Providence for turning the courses of fortune and actions of persons with whom we have any concern, so as to procure all the good intended to be bestowed upon us.

Nay further, when we consider that things visible and invisible, lie under the dominion of one governour, connecting

S all

Conclusion.

all in one wisely regulated polity, wherein nothing is established in vain, and reflect how much of our time is lost in sleep and infancy, how many pains, diseases and troubles fall upon us, how many unavailing hours pass over our heads, and how often we are forced to bestir ourselves to very little purpose of our own, there is a probable presumption that all these things turn some how or other to the account of other beings. So that our little concerns and transactions may be of greater importance than we imagine, and ourselves made unknowingly to work out the advantage of fellow-creatures, whereof we have not the least knowledge, nor even suspicion. Nor need we want hopes from the goodness of God, that we shall one day reap the benefit of those services wherein we have been made, tho' undesignedly, instrumental [a].

But

---

[a] I have already let the Reader into some of my good Cousin's fancies, which may be reckoned the luxuriancies of a warm imagination and contemplative turn: nor are such peculiar to him, but may be found among the ancient Philosophers, primitive Fathers, and modern Divines. In my third note on §. 20. I have hinted

Conclusion.

But how simple and confined, or how extensive and complicated schemes soever we hinted his notion, That all space not occupied by body, may be replete with spiritual substance; and that there may be other worlds created besides this we inhabit. When he talks of other worlds, he has not so much in his thoughts the supposition of earths and heavens beyond the starry sphere (though this too he does not deny) as other systems of creatures intermingled among our own; governed by distinct laws, yet ordered in such wisdom and contrivance, as not to disturb or interfere with those wherein we have concern.

My friend has some phlegm to temper his fire, which witholds him from catching at every plausible speculation carrying no appearance of benefit, but does not hinder him from embracing, perhaps too eagerly, whatever he conceives tending to display the divine Excellence, or raise our idea of the power, the wisdom, or the goodness of our Creator. Now it seems to him more glorious to those attributes, that there should be no desolate spot in the empire of God incapable of receiving his bounty, no stroke in his plan superfluous, nor work of his hand unproductive of uses proportionable to the largeness of the design; than that this immense fabric of the visible universe should be constructed only for the benefit of a few reptiles crawling about this insignificant globe; the greater part of whom have not even the benefit of contemplating the wonders it contains. Some perhaps may alledge, that profuseness gives the greater display of magnificence, as showing the inexhaustible riches of the divine power, so that God can afford an immense cost for the better accommodation of creatures whom he designs

we may conceive contained within the divine plan, the stumbling block of compulsion to favour. But let us consider why we esteem profusion a mark of magnificence in man; namely, because of his ignorance of the exact wants, and several likings of the persons he is to entertain; for could he know the precise measure of one, and particular objects of the other, he might give proof of his riches, by showing himself able to supply every man with what he desires, without heaping superfluities upon the table. Were we invited to the house of a great personage, where we saw preparations larger than could possibly contribute to our entertainment, should we not conclude that he had other guests to entertain besides ourselves? and did we perceive meats cooked up in a manner unsuitable to an *English* palate, should we not suppose he expected a company of foreigners, or persons whose palates were differently constituted from our own? By the same reason, when we behold mighty works in nature, which serve us only for objects of contemplation, may we not conclude there are other inhabitants whom they serve for more needful purposes?

As to those called by *Lucretius* the faults of Nature, however some righteous people may deny their being such, and insist that all things contribute in some shape or other, nearly or remotely, to our uses: my neighbour does not scruple to acknowledge there are faults, supposing man the sole object deserving regard. For though it might be difficult to point out a Reformation in any particular which would not be attended with worse inconveniencies, yet he thinks it too daring presumption to assert, that infinite Wisdom could not

have

Conclusion.

pulsion upon free Agency being removed, we may conclude that every purpose comprized have contrived methods for avoiding those inconveniencies, and formed a world better suited to the accommodation of human life, had that been the sole point in view. Therefore that this was not done, he looks upon as an evidence that there were other views to be provided for, and other creatures differently constituted, for whose advantage these seeming faults were calculated. Nor yet will he controvert, that all things we have knowledge of were made for the service of man, provided it be not added for man alone; for he observes, that nature serves many purposes by one and the same provision. The air we breathe wafts the birds aloft, sustains the vapours, and assists in the growth of vegetables: the woods, from whence we draw materials for ships, for houses, for utensils, for firing, afford shelter and pannage to the cattle, habitation and food to the fowls, harbour and nourishment to the insects. Why then should we imagine that multitude of immense bodies we see twinkle by night, were hung out only as a spectacle for us to gaze at? That the vast effusion of light was darted forth on all sides throughout the heavens, for the sake of a few rays to fall upon our eyes? That the boundless fields of Ether were spread out with no other design than for our little planets to roll in? To say this, he apprehends less worthy the divine attributes, and less agreeable to his favourite principle, of nothing made in vain, than to suppose innumerable hosts of perceptive beings, for whose conveniencies, and enjoyments, these stupendous works were contrived.

He remarks further, that universal Nature being the work of one Creator, and dominion of one Governor,

it

Conclusion.

prized therein has adequate causes provided for its execution, and every cause in act,

it is no unreasonable presumption to suppose it formed upon one all comprehensive plan, nor that the laws respecting the different systems of beings, are to be regarded as municipal, contained under one general polity: so that nothing stands alone, nor unconnected with the rest; but as other things were so far made for man as that regard was had to him in their establishment, so man was made for the service of his fellow-creatures, visible and invisible, regard being had to them in the constitutions of nature or fortune established for him, and his transactions, together with the incidents befalling him, being made productive of some advantages to them. He seems to see this notion confirmed by the constitution of things upon this sublunary stage, wherein men and animals, plants and elements mutually affect one another; from whence it may be presumed the like mutual affection prevails throughout the regions unseen. And as the profusion of stars, of light, and of ether, almost useless to us, give proof of other natures to whom they might be useful; so the waste of time, of thought, and labour, occasioned by sleep, by infirmities, error, and ignorance, which make large deductions from our enjoyment, must add as largely to it elsewhere.

He takes notice likewise, that nature forms her productions by long preparation, and through several steps: the little seed grows and ripens gradually in the pod of the flower; when falling into the ground, it shoots first a bud, then a stem, and lastly a full grown plant; and upon the structure of the embrio seed depend the kind, the qualities, the fruits of the future tree. Why then may not there be a like progression of

Conclusion.

act, whether voluntary or neceffary agent, contributes its fhare towards the completion of fome purpofe. Thereof the foul through her feveral forms of being; each being preparatory to the next, not only as our good or evil conduct here determines our condition either way hereafter, but as our feveral ways of living upon this ftage may fit us to perform different parts upon another? We have paffed through but one preexiftent ftate that we know of, I mean that of the womb, and upon what happened to us there, depends in great meafure our ftrength, our vigour, our genius, and our talents: nor does there want probability that the fame in our future birth will depend upon what has happened to us during our prefent ftate. For our fenfations pafs through the mental organization in their way to the mind: if I look upon a houfe, I have an image of it in my fancy, as well as when I think of it with my eyes fhut; and this image is neceffary to my perceiving it, for were I to ftare ever fo much while thinking intenfely on fomething elfe, I might have no more perception of the houfe than if there ftood none before me. But matter, however finely organized, can imprefs variety of Perceptions no otherwife than by being diverfly modified: whence it follows, that the action of our fenfes throws the mental organization into different modifications, and by doing this frequently, may bring the fibres of them into a different texture. Accordingly we find our habits, our turns of thought, our taftes, our feveral expertnefs in one way rather than another, formed in us by the objects wherewith we have been moftly converfant. So that every man's underftanding and imagination become diverfly modelled according as he has been a foldier, a fcholar, a mechanic, or a labourer. Now my contemplative and ferious friend, efteeming it for

the

Conclusion.

Therefore the doctrine of universal Providence being, as it seems to me, well established, the glory of God to discover new uses in the several provisions of nature, thinks this a presumptive evidence that the mind, or spiritual part, carries off this mental organization upon her departure; and that the professions whereinto we are diversly led, besides their uses in human life, adapt us severally for some peculiar functions we are destined to perform in our next form of being.

Nor does he scruple to imagine, that future punishments, may be derived through the same channel; human nature being so ordered, that the practice of vicious courses, by working improper mixtures into the organization, may render it disturbed and distempered, breeding the worm that dieth not, and the inward fire that is not quenched. For since nature is the work of God, and all her provisions of his contrivance, whatever misery shall follow by natural consequence is as much the effect of divine vengeance, as what is inflicted by the ministry of devils, or elementary flames.

When he reflects on the existence of evil, that mystery which the wit of man has never yet been able to unveil, he cannot allow any thing to exist necessarily, nor unproduced by the creator; therefore subscribes to what he apprehends a scripture doctrine, *That the Lord created evil as well as good.* Yet this work of the creation seeming repugnant to our ideas of infinite Goodness, he thinks we ought to extend it no further than experience and necessity oblige us; which justifies him in confining it to the embodied and inorganized states: so that when the spirit can get totally disengaged from matter, it shall become totally exempt

Conclusion.

established, I may go on without further scruple to raise what superstructure I can upon this foundation.

exempt from evil. This reduces the quantity of it within a very narrow compass, for bodies being extremely spongy, the most solid of them, upon *Newton*'s authority, containing more of pore than substance, he supposes that if all the matter within the solar system were compressed together, it would form a mass no bigger than the body of the sun. Therefore if all space be replete with spiritual substance, even admitting that so much of it as lies immersed in matter were constantly miserable (which God be thanked is far from the fact) the evil would bear no greater proportion to the good than the magnitude of that body to the whole system around it. So that it would be no extravagant figure to cry out with *David, Behold how high the heaven is in comparison of the earth, so great is the mercy of the Lord towards them that fear him!* Now to compute that proportion, reckoning the sun's diameter at 1200,000 miles, which the light, according to its volocity settled by *Newton*, would run over in seven seconds; and taking *Huygen*'s estimation of the distance of the nearest fixed star, which would require six lunar months for light to travel through: the sun's magnitude will be to that of his whole system, or the proportion of evil to good, as one to the cube of so many times seven seconds as are contained in the six months, that is, 89161004482560000000, almost nine millions of millions of millions.

Then being persuaded that God never terminates his purpose upon evil, nor sends it unless for some greater good to be brought out of it; he proceeds to examine in what manner it may be productive of good.

T   In

In order to this he confiders the nature of the mind, which never moves to action unlefs for avoidance of fome uneafinefs, or upon profpect of fome fatisfaction that would be loft without her endeavours to procure it: therefore a being poffeffed of happinefs, and in full fecurity that nothing could difturb or abate it, would remain in perpetual indolence, having no inducement to exert its activity. But the apprehenfion of evil fuffices to move the mind without its actually falling upon her, yet we cannot well conceive fuch Apprehenfion without actual fuffering fomewhere or other, and a very little will do for the purpofe; for one man's misfortune may give warning to a million, yet we fhould never have an apprehenfion of bruifes or broken bones, or other misfortunes, if they were never to happen at all; and perhaps a man who had never felt or feen any hurt, would wonder what you meant by admonifhing him to guard againft it. Therefore fome degree of actual fuffering may be neceffary to keep activity alive in the fpiritual fubftances for avoiding the fources of it. He thinks this the beft account that can be given for the origin of evil: and this affords a reafon why the heavenly bodies, together with the planetary fyftems probably furrounding them, were difperfed up and down to fuch immeafurable diftances, and the fields of ether ftretched throughout the vaft expanfe containing them; to wit, that the former might ferve as a habitation for animals, and the latter as a range for difembodied organizations; fo that famples of actual fuffering might not be wanted in any part of the univerfe.

Thus all nature ftands reciprocally connected: the purely fpiritual part having concern with the embodied, as exhibiting fpecimens of evil neceffary to preferve them in happinefs. And we having concern with
whatever

Conclusion.

whatever secures the happiness of those beings, among whom we hope one day to be incorporated.

These speculations, which he thinks helpful to open our minds, to give us a fuller idea of the divine bounty, magnificence, and polity, and a better opinion of that universal nature under whose laws we live, yet being of too thin and airy a nature to sink deep in the imagination; he has employed the hypotheses of vehicles, and a mundane soul, to render them more sensible and more easily retainable. For when a probable manner can be devised to shew how things may be effected, it gains them a readier reception than bare arguments to prove their reality. Nor are they new inventions of his own making: for many learned men have supposed an inner tunicle adhering to the mind upon her separation from the body; the antients painted the Soul, or Psyche, with butterflies wings, to denote her resemblance with a butterfly coming forth from the chrysalis in a body before formed therein; and St. *Paul* likens the spiritual body of resurgents to the blade springing from wheat, or barley, or it may be some other grain, which Naturalists tell us is no more than an expansion of the little germ contained in the seed. Nor can it be denied, that many of the old Philosophers held a mundane soul, or soul of the world, which though now commonly understood of the supreme Being, whoever examines their remains, will find they meant by it only a created substance, whereinto the souls of men and animals were absorbed.

These hypotheses effectually banish the notion of ghosts, apparitions, witchcraft, and the like. For the vehicles, although there be some unlucky malicious creatures among them, yet are too small and feeble to do us any mischief, or give motion to particles of matter enough to strike any of our senses. And the mundane

Conclusion.

mundane soul, although abundantly able to practise the art magic, and raise storms or earthquakes sufficient to beat our houses about our ears; yet is of too important a character to play tricks with us, and too great a lover of regularity ever to disturb the order of nature, or work any thing supernatural without an express direction from above.

Now should any body ask what use all these speculations are of, let him declare what he understands by use; if he means, for directing our measures in the common concerns of life, my honest Cousin readily acknowledges they are of none; therefore he would have them reserved for our closets, nor ever suffered to intrude upon our thoughts when we go about our ordinary transactions. But so neither are the articles of religion of any use upon these occasions: for who ever takes his measures in letting a farm, or buying a house, or ordering provisions for his family, from his opinion concerning the formation of the world, or a future state? Were I atheist or devotee, I should probably buy my wares at the same shop, and employ the same carpenter to mend the paling of my yard. Therefore let such as resolve to confine themselves to the daily business of their station, or to those courses of acting and thinking which custom has made current in the world, or who do not find these subjects suited to their taste, pass them over unheeded: yet they need not despise them for all that, until certain they can suit the taste, or uses, of nobody else. And if there be any who shall find my Author, or myself, have contributed the least towards enlarging or clearing his ideas, or improving his Theory of Providence, he is heartily welcome; nor shall either of us think the time we have spent for his serve ill bestowed.

F I N I S.

MAN in Queſt of HIMSELF:

OR, A

DEFENCE

OF THE

INDIVIDUALITY

OF THE

HUMAN MIND, or SELF.

Occaſioned by

Some REMARKS in the MONTHLY REVIEW for *July* 1763. on a Note in SEARCH's FREEWILL.

By CUTHBERT COMMENT, Gent.

They imagine Compounds to be ſomewhat really different from that of which they are compounded; which is a very great miſtake.
     Clarke, Attrib. 6th *Edit.* 1725. *page* 53.

Endleſly ſeparable parts are as really diſtinct Beings, notwithſtanding their contiguity, as if they had been at never ſo great a diſtance from one another.
     Ibid. p. 89.

LONDON:
Printed for R. and J. DODSLEY in *Pall-Mall.* 1763.
[Price One Shilling.]

Man in Queſt of Himſelf.

IT is an old obſervation, that nothing is more difficult for a Man to know than himſelf; inſomuch that this ſcience was thought unattainable without ſupernatural aſſiſtance; for

From Heaven's high dome deſcended, KNOW THYSELF.

But then this was underſtood to reſpect the knowledge of a Man's character, ſentiments, and real motives of action; nor was it ever eſteemed difficult to know his own perſon from that of another, or from his cloaths, his hair, or any thing elſe belonging to him. Whereas a difficulty has been lately ſtarted in aſcertaining what is properly *the Man*, or to what the pronoun *I* ought to be applied.

The laſt *Monthly Review* for *July* 1763. has made honourable mention of my Couſin and myſelf,

myself, and has interspersed therein some criticisms, by way of admonition for our conduct: He may see they are not lost upon us; for we have profited by them already in our title-page. We had proceeded before upon *Horace*'s antiquated rule, being studious rather of producing fire out of smoke, than smoke out of a flash; never reflecting, that since the invention of gunpowder it is manifest the gun can never do execution if the pan do not flash. So to please him, I have put a little more powder into the pan this time of charging: and we hope he perceives by the look of the flash, that our shot is not levelled against him, but against an opinion he has advanced. For these two are very different marks: people may differ in sentiment upon a speculative point, and still be very good friends. And indeed he has said so many obliging things of us, far beyond our most sanguine expectation, that it would be the height of imprudence to put him out of humour with us, or attempt to lessen his character: we rather wish his authority may be so great with the public, as that they may give their voices upon us according to his summing up the evidence; we shall be perfectly satisfied with the verdict.

Yet

Yet we shall observe in passing, that besides his admonitions, he has been careful to instruct us by his example too; for, though he has allowed my Author to have acquitted himself with politeness, yet it seems this was not a politeness of the right fashionable colour, admired in our great Metropolis and the adjacent Borough; therefore he has set us a pattern of the true genuine sort in the following expressions: *Greatly deficient in physiological knowledge;—Very considerable blunders;—These very accurate philologists;—Indeed, friend, you have here overlooked yourself;—It is with equal impropriety they talk.*—— Now, we must needs acknowledge these strains in the highest pitch of modern perfection, because the like abound in the *North Briton* and *Cave of Famine*, those celebrated performances, which every true-born Englishman doats upon. But we are much afraid whether we shall be able to copy after his example; for it is commonly observed, that nobody ever succeeds in a thing he does not give his mind to; but it happens unluckily that we find in ourselves no inclination to attain this modern genteelness: our ambition prompts us rather to the *Ridiculum* than the *Acre*, and we should be proud if we could acquire a spark of that old-fashioned ed politeneſs deſcribed by *Perſius* in one of his predeceſſors:

When Horace *every foible touch'd with art,*
His ſmiling friend receiv'd him to his heart,
Pleas'd with the tickling probe, nor felt it
    ſmart.
The teſty people too could patient ſtand,
While wip'd their follies by his ſkilful hand.

I don't know why he ſhould take ſuch diſtaſte at my button, unleſs perhaps that he ſaw his own face in one part of it; and might be a little chagrined to find, that I had not better maintained the dignity of the noble branch of the *Comments*:

However, I have the pleaſure to ſee this little diſappointment has not overcome his affection to a relation; for he has ſpoken of me in a very handſome manner, well becoming one *Comment* of another: and with reſpect to my Author, whom he will eaſily believe I muſt love as well as I do myſelf, he has proceeded with remarkable tenderneſs. For it being abſolutely neceſſary to find fault ſomewhere, becauſe the Public, proceeding for once upon a very right principle, That there can be no perſon nor performance in this world compleatly perfect, would not think him well

qualified

qualified for his office of Critic-General, if he did not find something to blame in every piece he took in hand; he has kindly spared the main work, and fallen upon one of my Notes, containing a matter no ways affecting the argument carried on in the text.

But notwithstanding his good intention, so it happens, that he has done us more mischief than we flatter ourselves he designed. For the Individuality of the Mind was a principle Mr. *Search* had depended upon to prove its unperishableness; which gave an opening to his enquiries concerning the other world. Because his plan having confined him to build solely upon the fund of natural reason, he was not entitled to avail himself of the assurances given in the Gospel: but while it remained uncertain whether our continuance was to last any longer than this life, there was very little encouragement to consider whether there were another world or no: on the other hand, if it could be shown from contemplation of our Nature, that the Mind is built to last for ever, then it would become expedient to examine what is likely to befal her hereafter, and whether any thing to be done at present may affect her future condition.

Therefore

Therefore my cousin exhorted me to endeavour settling what is a Man's Self, and whether it may have continuance after dissolution of the human frame: not in contradiction to Mr. *Monthly*, with whom we have no quarrel, but in defence of an article we conceive material, against whoever shall attack it, or as a further explanation to such as may not have fully comprehended our meaning.

But we must crave leave to make our defence in our own way: and as *Horace* observes that every animal places his dependence upon the arms Nature has furnished him with, the Wolf never defends himself with his heels, nor the Bull with his teeth: so we, who it seems are excellent Philologists, though greatly deficient in physiological knowledge, and for this reason do not clearly comprehend what is to be understood by physical and metaphysical existence, palpable and impalpable individuals, material and immaterial substance, as handled by our opponent, may be allowed to avail ourselves of that part where our greatest strength lies.

Therefore, under the guidance of our Patroness, who has helped us so well hitherto, we shall observe that *Same* is an equivocal term. If, upon giving me a glass of wine, I

should

should think it tasted different from that you gave me half an hour before, and you assure me it is the same wine, because you poured it out of the very same bottle, I should rest satisfied with the answer. But if a conjurer should pretend to take out a glass of wine unmingled that I had thrown into water, and upon his producing a glass of pure wine I doubted whether it were the same, if he should tell me, Yes, for he poured it out of the same bottle, I should think he trifled with me.

In like manner it may be said, that rich and poor are all the same flesh and blood, or that every stick of elder contains the same pithy substance. Yet whoever says this does not imagine, that my cookmaid and I have but one body, or the same mass of blood between us: nor that one stick of elder contains the same substance as twenty.

From hence we may see there are two sorts of identity; one wherein things are the same in appearance and quality, and this we may call specific: nevertheless they still remain numerically distinct; as this egg is not the same with that, how much soever it may be the same to the eye, or for any uses we may have of it.

Thus

Thus substances, as numerically distinguished, never fluctuate nor change into one another; their fluctuation is only of form or position upon their entering into compositions of substances specifically different. The same particles which were mould last year, might afterwards have become grass, then mutton, then human flesh, lastly, a flea or a maggot, and continue the same throughout all their several migrations: so that what is maggot now, may have been part of a man, or a sheep, or a blade of grass, or a clod of dirt.

Therefore if we consider man as the whole composition of flesh, blood, bones, and humours, it is plain he fluctuates and changes continually: for if he be kept without victuals, his substance wastes away, and is renewed again by proper nourishment: so that how long soever he may continue the same species of creature, he does not continue the same substance in all its parts a week nor a day. Nor was the Mr. *Monthly* who dealt so favourably with us in *July*, the same with him that treated a friend of ours with the like benignity in 1755.

I have met with some who say they have no idea of substance, because they cannot conceive one devoid of all quality whatever;

but

but this is not the right way of going to work for conceiving it. For there are some things we cannot apprehend exifting by themfelves, tho' we may eafily in conjunction with others: a father cannot be without a child; there cannot be colour without figure, nor figure without magnitude; yet the ideas of father and fon, of colour, figure and magnitude, are clearly diftinct. Nor, if we confider the matter fairly, is it more eafy to apprehend quality by itfelf than fubftance. For can there be fquarenefs without fomething fquare, or rednefs without any thing red? Or can there be a fquare or a red nothing, any more than a fubftance without quality? But fquarenefs and rednefs are only perceptions of the mind? What then? Should we fuppofe with *Berkeley*, (they are not effects of the external caufes we afcribe them to, then are there no qualities without us any more than there are fubftances: but if there be real qualities producing the perceptions, then is there a real fomething poffeffing the qualities. 'Tis true we may be fometimes deceived by appearances of things that are not real, as when a man fees apparitions: but tho' there be no fubftance ftanding before him in the place where he apprehends it to be, yet there is a real fubftance
fome-

somewhere, either in the eye, or the humours, or the brain, causing the appearance. Even in the most retired thoughts of the mind, whether we imagine her to raise these thoughts by her own immediate operation, then is she a substance possessing the quality of impressing them; or whether she uses some organ of our internal material frame, as an instrument to impress them by, then is the modification of that organ the object we discern.

But the strongest idea of substance we may have from ourselves, the knowledge whereof is more certain than that of qualities. For how know we the qualities are real, unless because we really perceive them? And if we are nothing real ourselves, they cannot be really perceived by us: for it is the hardest thing of all to conceive how any thing unreal can really do or be really affected by any thing. And this substance retains its existence when exerting no quality, as in sound sleep.

Qualities continually change: a square piece of clay may be moulded into a round, warm water may grow cold: but in all these changes something still remains the same, and that can be none other than the substance. When a

. quality

quality goes off, it is succeeded by another, as squareness in the clay by some other figure, and warmth in the water by coolness; nor does the substance ever want a quality to invest it: but the quality upon being altered does not fly off to some other substance, but is absolutely lost; and may be regained without being drawn from any other fund.

We come next to the term *Individual*; and what does that import but something that cannot be divided? therefore to talk of every Individual being a compound, is a palpable absurdity, a flat contradiction, the same as an indivisible divisible, or an uncompounded compound.—Perhaps here our Master will think us hopeful lads, beginning to come forward in the modern politeness: but we cannot arrogate so much merit yet; for we do not charge it upon him as a blunder or impropriety; and for this very good reason; because we could not do so without hitting ourselves a slap on the face. There were three young fellows once went to see a fine garden: one of them spying another pluck a peach, whispered the third, Pray is it right to take a Gentleman's fruit without leave? Yes, says he, it must certainly be right; because I have a couple in my pocket. So contraditradictions must sometimes be proper, because Mr. *Search* uses one in Page 12, where he says, " a man may have power when he has " it not." But then we see how he brings himself off by adding, " That is, he may " have it in one sense while he wants it in " another." Now if we take the same method for solving the other contradiction, perhaps we shall find it throw some light upon the argument in hand.

Naturalists (I beg pardon, I mean Physiologists) distribute the productions of Nature into kinds, as animals, vegetables, fossils; which they subdivide into Species, as Men, horses, sheep, &c. Several further divisions are occasionally made under these, as French, English, men grown, children, and the like. But you cannot go lower than the single bodies of each class, whose parts are joined together, not to be separated without losing their specific denomination, nor do we ever see them reunited after separation. Therefore we call them *Individuals*, because to us they appear such, and may be esteemed such for any uses we have of them.

Yet this manner of distribution admits of several exceptions: in some species there are no individuals, such as Fire, Water, Oil; because

cause in all divisions of them discernible by our senses, they still retain their specific qualities. Some individuals may be multiplied into many; an osier may be cut into twenty twigs, each whereof is a distinct plant of the same kind. Animals and vegetables receive their substance from parents of their kind, which substance nevertheless loses its species during the passage, and resumes it again afterwards: an egg is never numbered in species with the bird that laid it; but when hatched into a chicken, it ranks as one among the poultry. Both species and individuals are often made by art: Punch, Beer, and Mead are different kinds of liquor; and when a man takes an inventory of his houshold goods, he can distinguish those of the same sort only by individuals; or if he draws off a pipe of wine, he must drive in a cork to preserve each individual bottle from growing vapid. Thus we see that both in physiological and artificial estimation, *Individual* is an arbitrary term, applied to things for our convenience.

With regard to those species that have individuals, the term Existence or Being must belong to them. A Man, being I suppose a palpable Individual, will be allowed to have an Existence or Being of his own, distinct from

from all other men. So you will say the whole race of men has a Being and existence of its own, distinct from all other creatures. Very true: but not distinct from the men composing it; nor has it another Being to be added to the number of theirs. The same will hold good of any lesser collection of men; as a Regiment, which has not an additional Being over and above that of the men, nor exists otherwise than by their existence, which nevertheless they have independent on one another. For if Serjeant *Bluff* were annihilated, Corporal *Trim* might still continue the same Man he was: but if all the Men were annihilated, what would become of the regiment?

Nevertheless it is manifest that all these individuals, as our Corrector justly and properly expresses it, are compounds, consisting of parts substantially and numerically distinct from each other: so that the palpable substance, *Man*, is a collection of many substances, as the Regiment was; and has existence no otherwise than that; to wit, by the existence of his parts. Were his hands annihilated, his feet might remain the same Beings they were before, as *Trim* might upon the destruction

of

of *Bluff*; but were all his parts annihilated, the Man muſt utterly loſe his Being.

Well, but his hands and feet are compounds too, made up of the elements: therefore they have no other exiſtence than what belongs to the elements compoſing them. But what ſhall we ſay to theſe elements? for being a meer ignoramus in phyſiological knowledge, I proteſt I don't know what to make of them. I think I can feel earth, water, air, and fire, if they touch me in quantities enough to affect my ſenſes; therefore they ſhould be palpable. But we are told at firſt they are impalpable exiſtencies; and yet I am not ſure of that neither; for it is ſaid afterwards, that if they fluctuate and change into one another, they are no exiſtencies at all, being devoid not only of palpable, but of abſolute and metaphyſical exiſtence, which belongs to nothing beſides God alone.

I ſhall not deny it poſſible the elements may change into one another, but then this is a fluctuation of form, or of eſſence, which ſeems all along to have been miſtaken for exiſtence, not of ſubſtance: for it is impoſſible to conceive any particular ſubſtance ſhould ever change into another ſubſtance, whether ſimilar or of different kind. An egg, by putrefaction

faction and vegetation, may in procefs of time become an apple; but this egg can never become that egg, nor that apple; nor can either egg or apple ever lofe their numerical exiftence, whatever various forms they pafs thro', or new effences they take. So if what now is earth once was water, ftill it is the fame fubftance diverfly modified: nor can this drop of water ever be turned into that drop, or that fpeck of dirt, by any fluctuation whatever.

But if the elements may change, it muft be by a various difpofition of their parts; therefore they have parts: and I fuppofe it is underftood, tho' not expreffed, that thefe parts have under parts, and fo on for ever. Which *fubintelligitur* is neceffary to prove the non-exiftence of elements: for fince they be compounds, having no other exiftence than that of their parts, nor thefe than of the under parts compofing them, we cannot make them a title to exiftence, until we come to abfolute Individuals without any parts at all, which it is fuggefted, are no-where to be found.

Before this was urged againft us, it fhould have been remembered what antagonifts we were contending with, namely, the Stratonic and Democritic Atheifts, who would not have

preffed

pressed us so closely: for they admitted Atoms absolutely indivisible, whereout the souls of men, and all other productions were formed; and held, that these Atoms were floating about in infinite space, distinct and separate from each other, until by their collisions, assortments, and adhesions, they ranged themselves into the compound bodies we see. Upon this hypothesis, it is plain there was the same number of substances from all eternity there is now; and upon their clustering together, whether by chance or necessity, nothing new, unless in kind and quality, or essence, not in substance, could be produced. Therefore the souls of Men could have no distinct existence of their own, nor other than that of the Atoms composing them: and upon their dissolution, not a single Being would be lost; any more than the King would lose a subject, that is, a palpable substance, upon disbanding a regiment.—Nevertheless these Atoms were a sufficient foundation for the existence of what they composed, their substance being that of the compounds whereinto they entered. So that our argument, however defective in proving our point to other people, may still remain good *ad hominem*, upon the occasion whereto we applied it.

Yet

Yet we need not want the like foundation without availing ourselves of the Atheist's concession: for after all possible division of Matter, it will continue Matter still; nor can you reduce it to nothing by any separation of parts whatever; whence it follows, that there are particles which never were, nor ever will be smaller than they are. These then may fairly be stiled Atoms actually, if not potentially, indivisible. Nor is this repugnant to the opinion now generally received among physiologists, that all Matter is homogeneous; all compound bodies being made up of a *Materia prima*, which is every where one and the same in kind and quality, their various essences resulting from the various assortments whereinto it is cast.

If it be said the particles of *Materia prima* must have a right side and a left, separable, tho' perhaps never actually separated from one another; this is more than we are warranted to assert. For the most considerate persons have forborn to pronounce peremptorily upon the divisibility of matter, any further than that it is indefinite, that is, no magnitude can be assigned than which we may be assured there cannot be a smaller. But divisibility absolutely infinite, has its difficulties as well as finite:

for

for upon that hypothefis, half an apple muft contain as many parts as the whole; for the half containing infinite parts, nothing can be greater than infinite; yet the other half containing the like infinity, to fay that the addition of them does not encreafe the number in the whole, feems as abfurd as to deny that two and two make four. Since then we have not faculties to determine this point with certainty, the evidence before us of bodies exifting, and of their having no further exiftence beyond that of their parts, is a ftronger proof that a ftop muft be put to divifibility fomewhere, tho' we cannot tell where, than our want of conception of a particle without fides is of the contrary. For neither our fenfes nor imagination can go beyond a certain degree of minutenefs; how then do we know what we might fee or apprehend, were they acute enough to difcern or comprehend objects below that degree.

However this be, it can fcarce be doubted that the matter, or firft principle of bodies, has an exiftence of fome fort or other, whether original or derivative, 'tis no matter; and that whatever higher compofitions are formed thereout, exift only in the exiftence of that; becaufe if the matter of any body were annihilated,

hilated, the exiftence of that being withdrawn, the body would be no more. Juft as a Regiment exifts only by the exiftence of the men, of whatever kind it be belonging to them, and upon their annihilation could exift no more.

But it is alledged, that a Regiment has no Being. Why? Becaufe all compounds, according to us, have no exiftence at all. Pray when did we ever fay fo? Did you never hear of the Welfhman, who riding with a heavy portmanteau before him, and perceiving his horfe tire, took up the portmanteau upon his own fhoulders to eafe the beaft? never confidering that while the horfe carried him that bore the burthen, he carried that too : and if there had been twenty men hoifted upon one another, fo long as the uppermoft had the portmanteau upon his fhoulders, the horfe would have carried the fame weight as if it had lain upon his own back. So while the component parts of bodies exift, their exiftence runs thro' the compofitions whereinto they enter; and palpable Individuals, together with whatever Companies, Regiments, Corporations, or other Compounds can be formed of them, have as much exiftence as their primary principles, becaufe they have the very fame.

There-

Therefore we never denied a Regiment to have exiftence or Being; but only that it was a Being in the fingular number, diftinct from that of the men, and to be added to them.

We conceived it to be like a noun of number, as a Grofs, a Score, a Dozen, which, tho' *entia rationis* in themfelves, yet have a real exiftence when applied to particular fubftances. For a dozen of counters exift as really as a fingle one; if you put the dozen into your pocket, you put in real fubftance, not a fhadow or meer imagination; yet you have not thirteen things there, to wit, twelve counters and the dozen over and above.

You fay, if a regiment is no Being, neither is man a Being; and this you charge upon us as an egregious overfight. But upon what principles does the confequence follow? Why, upon thofe of the Atheifts we were combating; and was fo far from being an overfight, that the main ftrefs of our argument lay in driving our Antagonifts to the abfurd conclufion of making man to have no Being, no diftinct exiftence peculiar to himfelf; nor any thing more than a regiment of atoms, admirably well marfhalled and difciplined indeed, but fubftantially and numerically the fame they were before enlifting.

Upon

Upon our own principles the conclusion runs the other way: for we argue, that Man must be an Individual, not like your palpable Individuals, consisting of parts, because he has a Being of his own. And for the truth of our *postulatum*, we appeal to every man, Whether he can doubt of his own existence, or that he has a personality distinct from that of all other Beings.

Nevertheless this appeal, it seems, cannot avail us; because, how could any man acquire this sense or knowledge of his personality without a human body? or in other words, how can a man exist without a body? Had we said the mind or soul of man might so exist, it would have been less exceptionable; and yet exceptionable it would have been; for how could the mind acquire a sense of personality without a body? Now if it be remembered what was the opinion we set out to battle against in the beginning of my note, namely, that the souls of men, as well as all other productions, were formed out of atoms, the correction of Man into Mind might have been spared. For when afterwards we spoke of the atoms running together to compose a human body, we thought that, upon the principles of our adversaries, Mind and Body must be the same thing:

thing: but if any one thinks otherwise, he is welcome to *dele* Body, and read Mind, Soul or Spirit; our argument will run never the worse.

As to the question, whether a Man or a Mind can acquire a sense of personality without a human body; we apprehend it as difficult for any body to answer in the negative, as for us in the affirmative. It may be said indeed, as is said of Mr. *Locke*, that the negative may be very easily proved on our own principles: certainly nothing is more easy than to assert this, and it may pass with such Readers as will take positiveness for demonstration: but it may not be quite so easy to make out the assertion.

But supposing it certain there can be no knowledge of personality without a body, how does it follow that no personality or existence can be had without one? or that not having knowledge of existence, and not existing, are synonimous expressions? This is new doctrine to us, and the logic by which it is proved, rises far above our pitch. It puts us in mind of that used in our infancy under the dictates of pure nature, unperverted by education, when the child hides its face in Mamma's apron, and then cries, *Nobody sees me.*

me. Which, in the learned language of our Cenfor, would run thus, " In this fituation I " can acquire no fenfe or knowledge of any " body's feeing me; therefore, or in other " words, nobody does fee me.". Now in our humble apprehenfion, the reality of a fact is not the fame thing with the evidence of it: the one may be true, tho' the other be wanting. If we have evidence of a thing's exifting, we may believe it had an exiftence before we knew it, and may ftill continue to exift after our evidence is withdrawn and loft out of our memory.

I doubt not Mr. *Monthly* has paffed many a night in found fleep, fince he did us the honour to take notice of us; for, confidering how much more than juftice he has done our characters in the principal parts of them, he can have had nothing to difturb his reft upon that fcore. Then during all thefe naps, I fuppofe he had no fenfe or knowledge of his own exiftence: but will he therefore fay, that he really had no exiftence? or that every time he fell afleep, he ceafed to be, was no Perfon, no Subftance, no Being? but refumed all thefe again the moment he awoke in the morning? Therefore upon what grounds can he infer, that when he, and we, and all hu-

man

man palpable Individuals shall become stupified in the sleep of death, we shall utterly lose our existence, tho' we lose all evidence of it; and that a new set of corporeal organs (if such organs be necessary) may not invest and awaken us to a new scene of evidence?

What shall we say of the houses, the trees, the fields we see around us? have they a knowledge of their existence? or do they therefore not exist at all? To draw this consequence, must drive us plumb into *Berkley*'s scheme; that bodies subsist only in our idea, and are, or cease to be, according as our ideas fluctuate. So that when every body goes out of the room, the tables, the chairs, the pictures, they left behind, become instantly annihilated; and upon the company's return, become as instantly re-existent.

Notwithstanding all this, he will not deny that the mind or spirit of man may be an individual existence, to be destroyed only by the immediate exertion of Omnipotence. Yet in effect he does deny it a few lines below; for he says, that by existence, in this case, must be meant an absolute and metaphysical existence; in which sense it is more than probable, there is no other Being in the universe but God: for while every thing in nature appears to be in a constant fluctuation and change, it is rational enough to suspect, from analogy, that even the elements of things may be so too. Now this reasoning seems to imply, that the spirit of man is no more than a fifth element, like that called by *Aristotle*, *Entelechia*; for unless the mind be included in the elements, the argument from their fluctuation, that there is no created substance metaphysically existing, would not hold good: or that it is something analogous to the spirit of brandy or hartshorn, a drop of which being put into *Tunbridge* water, takes off the chill it would else cast upon weak stomachs; so a drop of the spirit of man infused into his material composition, takes off the insensibility naturally belonging to it, and renders it capable of sense and understanding. Yet it is plain, this drop may be divided into parts, which may one after another enter into the composition of the other elements: so that what is now spirit of man, may by and by become a drop of water, a puff of air, a spark of fire, or a speck of earth.

If this be so, I see no reason for calling in Omnipotence to destroy the spirit of man; for I suppose there are certain stated laws, I must not say of nature, but, of the universe, operating

rating these fluctuations and changes of the elements. And that the changes must be gradual we may presume from analogy; for tho' a dead dog may become a tree by being buried under it, it must putrify first, and be reduced to something which is neither animal nor vegetable substance, before it can be drawn up by the radical fibres of the tree. So the elements, during their passage into one another, must be no elements at all, neither earth, nor water, nor air, nor fire, nor *entelechia*, and consequently be non-existent; for palpable existence they have none, and other existence, we are told, belongs not to created things.

The result of all this is, that ourselves, and whatever we see or handle, are made up of non-entities, than which nothing can be harder of digestion; and if we can pronounce any thing, we may pronounce this absolutely impossible even to Omnipotence. I have heard indeed, that God created all things out of nothing, but I never knew it understood thereby, that he employed Nothing as a material whereout to fabricate his worlds; or that he moulded and kneaded up a certain quantity of Nothing, as a baker kneads his dough, until it became Something. I know the Atheists, *Lucretius* in particular, charge this idea of creation

creation upon us, and take great pains to overthrow it; but they fight all the while with a fhadow; for no Theift ever entertained fuch a notion.

Another reprehenfion given us is for faying, that upon diffolution of the human body, there is not a Being loft out of Nature; which expreffion, *Out of Nature*, is, it feems, fuch an egregious impropriety, as to deferve being ftigmatized with *Italics*. But we were unwaringly drawn thereinto by the example of other perfons before us: for we have heard of there being a God in Nature—of invifible Natures, perhaps more elegantly expreffed by impalpable Natures—of the Nature of virtue, juftice, government, and many other things which are not objects of phyfiological knowledge. And if we were led to talk like children, by converfing among other children, it had been kind in our Mafter to have inftructed us how to fpeak with better propriety: for he might know well enough that our meaning was only to affert, that upon certain fubftances joining together in a compound, there is not a new Being added to the number upon compofition, nor is one loft again out of the whole number upon feparation. Now how ought we to have expreffed ourfelves upon on this occafion? In fhort, it feems not very material whether we add *Out of Nature*, or omit it. If a billet be confumed in the fire, we fuppofe the parts of it are diffipated, but not annihilated: a few of them only remain palpable in the afhes, but whether the reft be in nature or out of nature 'tis no matter, fo they be exiftent fomewhere; there will ftill be the fame number of parts as before difunion; and the billet having no exiftence over and above, or diftinct from the parts, there will not be a Being loft upon its confumption. But we muft correct our theory againft another time, and adopt a new article of Faith, to wit, that a compound may confift of parts which had no exiftence in Nature before they entered into it; and the five elements themfelves, for we muft reckon the *Entelechia* for one, be made up of a *Materia prima*, every where uniform, and capable of being formed into any of them indifferently, tho' there be no fuch thing in Nature as a *Materia prima*.

Yet we cannot help faying, it was a little ungenerous in Mr. *Monthly* to attack us in flank, while we were engaged with another enemy, againft whom our difpofition was not improperly made: for they being as deficient in phyfiology as ourfelves, would not have denied

nied the existence of atoms in nature; therefore we still humbly conceive it was with propriety with respect to them we urged, that after dispersion of the atoms, there must be as many Beings in nature, as there had been during their coalition in a man. And consequently, if Man has a Being and Personality of his own, distinct from all other Beings, and which would be lost out of Nature upon his annihilation, he cannot be such a compound of atoms.

But having driven them out of the field, and being now to deal with another kind of assistant, we may be allowed to change our disposition according to the nature of the attack.— But hold: we shall be chid again: for *Attack* is not a physiological Being, and there may be great impropriety in applying the term *Nature* to it. Well then, according to the manner of the attack. For atoms, it seems, there are none, and the principles of physical Beings have no existence in nature, until formed into compounds. Let us try then how we can manage our argument by help of physical Beings alone: and in so doing, our example of the regiment may still serve our purpose. For the men are admitted on both sides to be substances, whether palpable or metaphysical, whether individual

vidual or compound, 'tis all one; for though we love hair-splitting as well as most folks, where necessary, we see no use for it here: Substances they still are, distinct and independent on one another. If then there were six hundred of them dispersed about the country, they did not, upon being incorporated into ten Companies and one Regiment, become six hundred and eleven substances: nor will the King, upon disbanding them, lose a single Subject, or Substance, or Being, out of his dominion. For surely disbanding is not annihilating, nor can you conceive any Existence or Substance belonging to the Regiment annihilated so long as the men remain all alive.

Now, to apply this to man: if he be a compound, yet we are not obliged to go so far as to the primary principles whereof his elements are constituted, for then we shall wander out of Nature; but we may distribute his whole composition into parts still remaining palpable, as his arms, his legs, his heart, his brain; suppose twenty of them. These twenty parts then are so many several Beings, numerically and substantially distinct from each other in the composition; for the leg is not the arm, nor the brain the heart, even in a living man. So that he is nothing more than a Regiment or collection of thefe twenty parts, having no diftinct Being of his own which might be added to theirs to make the whole number twenty-one. And if they were feparated by diffection, though they would lofe their vitality, they would not lofe their fubftance, but there would ftill remain twenty fubftances, as many as could be counted in the whole compofition, nor would a fingle Being be loft out of Nature.

Therefore if a man, while poffeffing his fenfes and underftanding, has undoubted evidence of his own exiftence and perfonality diftinct from all other Beings, and adds one to the number of thofe exiftent, he cannot be a compound or collection of fubftances, but an individual, making fome one particular part of the compofition whereinto he enters.

This brings us to the examination of what is properly a Man's Self, or that whereto the perfonal pronouns *I*, *You*, *He*, and *She*, may be applied. And here perhaps at firft there may be thought to be no difficulty; for upon a man coming into the room, my eyes may inform me fufficiently of his perfon, and I may fee plainly enough that he is not the table, the chairs, nor the wainfcot furrounding him. Very well: let us try then what I can difcover

by

by my eyes. Why, I fee a face, a pair of hands, a coat, ftockings, and fhoes: are all thefe *You?*———No to be fure: You know well enough I pull off my coat and fhoes when I go to bed, and put on banyan and flippers in the morning.——— Well, but you don't pull off your hair and nails when you go to bed: then they are parts of *You.*———No, no: they are only excrefcencies; for they have no fenfe or feeling.———How fo? If any body was to tear off a parcel of your hair, or one of your nails, fhould not you feel a grievous fmart?———Ay, the pronoun *I* fhould, becaufe they are faftened to my flefh; but the hair and the nails would feel nothing. They are like a packthread wound round my wrift, which if any one fhould twitch violently, he would hurt the wrift, but he would not hurt the packthread,———So then what has fenfe and feeling only is *Yourfelf.*———Undoubtedly: and every thing that has fo is a part of *Myfelf.*——— What think you of your teeth, your bones, your fat, the humours in your glands? for alterations may happen in them without your feeling it.———I don't know what to fay to that: for in common acceptation every thing is reputed *Myfelf* that remains with me after I have pulled off all my cloaths, except the ex-

E 2 crefcencies.

crefcencies.———Ay, and the excrefcencies too fometimes: for we often defcribe a man's perfon by the colour of his hair; and fhould do by his nails, if they have any thing remarkable or diftinguifhing; nay, by his cloaths, if we think he has but one fuit to wear. So you fee the term *Self*, like other terms of common acceptation, is fluctuating, determined this way or that by the prefent occafion: for he that, upon his knife flipping while he carves a loin of mutton, is afked whether he has cut himfelf, may fay, No, 'tis only a piece of my nail; but if he dafhes the gravy upon his coat, he will be apt to fret at having greafed himfelf. But what do you take to be truly and properly *Yourfelf?*———I doubt I muft give up the bones, the fat, and the humours: but furely my fyftem of nerves, and organs of fenfe, muft be *Myfelf*; for the great Mr. *Monthly* pronounces, that without them I could not have knowledge of my perfonality, or, in other words, could not exift.———But then it is the nerves and organs jointly that make *Yourfelf*. Your eyes are not *You*, nor your ears, nor your brachial or crural nerves; but the whole compofition of them altogether is that whereto the pronoun *You* belongs.———So it fhould feem.———Suppofe an Englifh foldier has loft a leg in Germany,

many, may he afterwards say, I was born in England:——Why not?—Becaufe the palpable compound *born*, to which the pronoun *I* was then applicable, is now no more, being deftroyed by fubtraction of the nerves in the leg.———Oh! but it is ftill a part of the fame compound.——Remember what you faid before, that it was not your eye, nor your ear, but the whole compofition which was *Yourfelf*.— But it is rational enough to imagine from analogy, that compounds may fluctuate and change into one another, fo that what was a Self with two legs may become a Self with only one. —May be fo: but then it is not the fame Self; for the term *Self* belonging to the whole compofition, it is plain the prefent compofition wants a part which was an ingredient helping to complete the former.——You puzzle me now. I wifh Mr. *Monthly* were here: I warrant he would manage yon with a wet finger. And yet I cannot help thinking the man was the fame Self after lofing his leg as before, and might apply the pronoun *I* to whatever was done or fuffered by the two-legged Self.—— Take care. For if the Self remains entire after lofs of the leg, then it will follow that the leg, while in vital union with the body, was no conftituent part of the palpable fubftance *I*;

becaufe

because this suffers no diminution by the amputation. But we will not press this, because you have not your champion by to help you out.

Therefore let us take the compound before fluctuation, while the man has all his limbs and senses entire. In this state I suppose the whole composition, not any part, nor any number of parts less than all, is *You:* so that what the composition does, you do; and, *vice versa*, whatever is done by you is done by the whole composition.——You are right.——Pray do you hear me speak?——Why should you ask? have not I answered you all along?—— I am not sure of that: Something has heard and answered me all along very clearly: but I am in some doubt whether that was *You*; because it seems to me not to have been your whole composition. Did your eyes hear any thing of what I said?——They helped to understand you, by observing your gestures, and motion of your lips.——Probably they might: But had your nose or the nerves of your legs or arms any share in the hearing?—— There was no occasion: for I have ears good enough to perform the office of hearing without other aid.——So your ears, or if you please to add eyes, have performed the whole office

office of hearing and underſtanding; and I have been talking all this while, not with your whole compoſition, nor with *You*, but with a pair of eyes and ears.——Pſhaw! now you joke with me. And let me tell you, this does not fit ſo eaſy upon you, nor appear ſo little forced as your argument. Can any body deny that what my ears hear is my hearing?—I deny or affirm nothing; I only aſk, whether what your eyes ſee, and your ears hear, is ſeen and heard by your whole compoſition?——I think it is. I am ſure it is ſeen and heard by *Myſelf*: for I have no notion of one Self to ſee, another to hear, another to ſmell, and ſo on; nor of half Myſelf ſeeing when the other half does not. But to my thinking a perception received at any one part runs through the whole Self, the whole compoſition.—-—Does it ſo? When you look at a picture, does the ſight of it run down to your great toe? and when ſomebody treads upon your toe, do your eyes inſtantly feel a ſympathetic ſmart?—I am ſure it is the ſame *I*, the ſame *Self*, that ſee the one and feel the other.——Then if you have but one Self to ſerve you upon all occaſions, and this Self cannot perceive by halves, muſt it not be ſomething diſtinct from the nerves and organs, which alternately remain inſenſible of one another's other's perceptions? And is it not rational enough to fuspect, that thefe organs are only channels of conveyance tranfmitting their refpective notices, as windows tranfmit the light, to the fame Self, the whole of which perceives every thing that is perceived?———O! for Mr. *Monthly* again, to ftand by and fee my head broke! But fuppofing it were fo; may not this *Self* be ftill a compound?———I am afraid we fhall hardly be able to make a palpable individual compound of it: fo we have loft our exiftence already; for nothing it feems exifts that is not fo, nor is there any thing individual unlefs compounds. Nor do I much care: for, fo we can find pleafure in one another's company, it is no matter whether we find it with exiftence or without. But what do you take this compound to be?———Truly, I don't very well know: but fuppofe it to lie fomewhere in the brain. We are told the nerves have been traced to the pineal gland: perhaps there may be a drop of the fifth element; or fpirit of man, gathered there; and then that is the *Self* whereto the perfonal pronouns belong.———

Do you apprehend yourfelf to be a real Being, or only a dream, a mere fancy or imagination? ———I cannot doubt of my exiftence, fo long as

as I have my senses.——— The having your senses depends upon your having sensitive organs, which we have now agreed are no parts of you, therefore are separable from you. But upon such separation should you lose your Being, because you lost the knowledge or consciousness of it?——— No, provided the drop remained entire.——— Suppose the drop, without being ever dissipated, should get into the pineal gland of another human body, should you regain your knowledge and consciousness?
——— I should know I had a Being, but not that I was the same Being and Person I am now, because probably I might not remember any thing passing with me now.———
Well, but tho' you might not know it, should you not really be the same Person and Being?
———Certainly: for the drop being Me, while that remains the same, I must be the same.———
So the Being and Substance of the drop are your Being, which you undoubtedly know you possess, while you have your senses.——— They are———And the materials of the drop are your materials.———Yes.———Do you and the drop make two Beings?——— No: both are one and the same.——— So while the whole drop continues to subsist, you subsist.———I do.———
But the drop may be divided into two half drops.———Ay, and those again into infinite parts;

parts; for Matter is divisible *ad infinitum.*—— With all your divisions, can you ever reduce it to nothing?——I do not pretend that.——Is there not the same substance or quantity of matter in the two halves as there was in the whole drop?——To be sure.——And after their being divided into infinite parts, is there not still the same quantity among them all?——I agree it.——Then none of your substance being lost, you still continue to subsist, notwithstanding an infinite dissipation of your parts. —— My Substance does; but not Me.—— Why so? Are you any thing else than the substance whereof you consist?—— Yes, the union of it into a compound is necessary to my subsistence.——Is Union a substance?—— I never said it was.——Can it make a substance?——It may make that to be one which was many before.——Is that one any addition to the number there was before union, or has it any other existence besides or over and above theirs?——

It does not to the number of substances, but it has an existence besides theirs.—— How do you make that out?—— Because, in common propriety of speech, we apply existence to the composition distinct from the substances compounded. — In what instances, pray? — Some people deny there is any such thing as a circle

existing

exifting in nature; for what appears fuch, they fay, is only a Polygon whofe angles are imperceptible. Now when they fay this, they do not mean to deny the exiftence of the bodies feeming to be circular: and if they admit the exiftence of fquares and triangles, thefe are different ideas from that of the fubftances exifting in them.——Different ideas they may be without being different exiftencies: for compofition may ftill be no more than a particular mode of exifting in fubftances, upon their coming into union from being difperfed. And it is not neceffary that upon their being caft out of a triangle into a fquare there fhould be an exiftence loft and gained, but only that they change their manner of exiftence, which whether in fquare or triangle is ftill their exiftence, not that of any thing elfe.——Still, in my apprehenfion, when a thiftle grows out of the ground, there is a plant in being which was not exiftent before.——Well, if you make a difficulty, we do not love contefting where it is needlefs. We will fuppofe Compofition to have an exiftence diftinct from the fubftances compounded.——Thank ye, for your indulgence. Tho' I am afraid you would not grant it, if you thought it would do me any good.——It could do you no good to deny it. Upon this fuppofition there will arife a new queftion, What is properly

perly You, and your Exiftence? for you know you have one of fome fort or other: whether it be the exiftence of your compofition with that of your fubftance jointly, or the former alone abftracted from the latter.——Stay; I muft think a little: this is not a matter to be determined prefently.——Nay, if you are not clear, never ftand to puzzle your brains about it. For whichever way we take it, our argument will run the fame: fo we will try with the Compofition, confidered apart from the materials united by it.——Take your own way, fince you fay both will conduct to the fame point.——Lay down a brafs quadrant upon the table: I fuppofe you will allow it has a compofition exifting diftinctly from all other compofitions.——Very readily.——Place another equal quadrant of filver by it. Has not that a compofition of its own exifting too?——Certainly.——Does it deftroy the compofition of the other?——How can it affect that, only by being laid fide by fide by it?——Put two other quadrants of fteel and copper againft the former: Have not the four fo many diftinct compofitions exifting in them?——No doubt they have.——But all together make a compleat circle.——True.——Has not this circle a compofition too? ——Undoubtedly.——Is the compofition

position of the circle any thing elfe than an aggregate of the four compofitions in the quadrants?——Nothing elfe, that I know of. ——Now let us return to the human body. Has not your right leg a compofition of its own diftinct from that of your left?—It has. ——And your right arm another?—Yes.—— And your nofe another?——To be fure.—— And every part of your human frame a feparate compofition of its own.——I cannot deny it.——But we difcovered before, that the parts I have named were no parts of *Yourfelf*.——We muft not retract that :——So your exiftence lies in the compofition of the drop or fpirit of man lodged in your pineal gland.——It does. ——Which drop may be divided into two halves.——It may.——And each of thefe halves into three hundred fubdivifions.—-Ay, fo many at leaft.——And matter being divifible *ad infinitum*, each of thefe fubdivifions are compounds having a compofition exifting in them diftinct from all the reft.——Admit that they have.——Then is the compofition of the drop, which is *You*, any thing elfe than the aggregate of the fix hundred compofitions in the fubdivifions?——It muft be fo : *Plato,* thou reafoneft well.——So now we are come to the regiment again. This plaguy trouble-
fome

some foe pursues us to whatever quarter we can turn, and drives us to a concession, that we have no better title to existence than itself; and it appears in all lights that you have no distinct Being of your own, being nothing more than a regiment or collection of infinite substances or existencies; and upon the disbanding of them, tho' you cease to be, yet there is not a Being, a Compound, a Composition, lost out of the universe.——Yet for all that I cannot help thinking, that upon my ceasing to be, there must be one Being the fewer in the universe: so I shall suppose, that so long as the substance composing me subsists, however dispersed or dissipated, I shall subsist.

But this will avail us little: for bare existence without perception is of no value; and when the particles fall out of their union and intercourse with one another, they cannot form a perceptive compound.—— That's a great comfort, no doubt: But supposing any of them could see, or hear, or feel, while you subsist, and they continue to be parts of you, tho' dispersed to great distances; should you be insensible of their perceptions?—— Supposing that, I must be affected with what affects any of them: but this an impossible supposition, because they cannot perceive unless

in

in compofition.—— But after being decompounded they may come into compofition again.—- Poffibly they may.—- The elements perpetually fluctuate and change: fo what is now fpirit of man, may become fpirit of brandy, and in further procefs of time may become fpirit of man again, either in one compofition, or interfperfed among feveral drops gathered in feveral pineal glands.——I cannot deny the poffibility of this.—— Then in this ftate of compofition they will all be perceptive, but probably have very different and contrary perceptions; fome feeing while others do not fee, fome being in pleafure while others are in pain. And as you muft be affected with whatever affects them, you muft then have thefe contrary perceptions at the fame time, and enjoy pleafure while you fuffer pain.—— I can't tell how to come into this notion tho', that I may fee and not fee, be in pleafure and pain at the fame inftant.——

You know the almighty power of Chance, and how in the courfe of infinite ages fhe muft produce all poffible combinations. Now one poffible combination is this; that fome thoufands of years hence half your drop and half mine fhould join in one pineal gland, and the other halves in fome other pineal gland.

Will these two compounds be Persons having knowledge of their own existence?——I make no doubt of it.———Will they be distinct and different persons from one another?———Certainly.———Which of them will be one of us? ———Neither.———Do not we subsist so long as our substances subsist; and shall not we perceive whatever they or any parts of them perceive?———We agreed so just now; not in liking to the hypothesis, but because drove out of every other.———Shall we have any other substance, or existence, or perception, than what belongs to those two Persons?——— And yet I can never bring myself to believe that I can become another Person, or part of another Person, or perceive by his perceptions, much less by the perceptions of two.———

So long as you continue alive, I suppose, you are the same Person you were some years ago. You can agree to this without being drove out of all other hypotheses.——— Very readily. Nobody can doubt that.——The same Being, Existence, or individual Substance.——— Certainly. And the same individual Compound too.——— Do not the humours of our body continually fluctuate and change, being first secreted from the blood, then entering into the substance of our flesh, and afterwards flying

off

off by perspiration?——— One cannot be ignorant of this, without great deficiency in physiological knowledge.——— Is it not rational enough to suspect from analogy, that the spirit of man (if it be a fifth element, or material fluid) fluctuates in like manner; being first secreted from the animal spirits, then turning to the medullary substance of the brain, and afterwards flying off by perspiration?——Truly there is a shrewd suspicion of such analogy.— And as the particles of this fluid are detached, others flow in to supply their places; so that there may not be one particle the same that was there some time ago: but what is now spirit of man in you, once was blood, or chyle, or victuals you have eaten, and perhaps a twelvemonth hence may be vapour floating about in the air; yet *You* continuing all the while the same substance and person.—I don't know how to disprove all this.———Then if *You* are a real Being and Substance, and are not barely a form or mode of existence in something else, and if your Existence and Personality remains the same throughout all the stages of life, from infancy to extreme old age, notwithstanding all the changes of particles in your drop; may we not argue, as we did before, concerning the nerves and the organs,

G that

that they are no parts of *You*, but channels to convey perception to something else, which is numerically and substantially *Yourself?*—— Well, I'll say no more, but turn you over to my champion.

Thus which ever way we turn ourselves, we find nothing but absurdity and contradiction, so long as we place our existence and personality in a compound: nor can we escape them otherwise than by admitting an Individual, not one of your compound individuals, which is none at all except in idea, but an Individual truly such, consisting of no parts; that cannot either totally or partially become another substance, nor can lose its identity unless by annihilation: in which case there would be a Being absolutely lost out of Nature, that is, out of the number of Beings existent. Into whatever composition this Individual enters, we esteem it *Ourselves* for the time, notwithstanding any fluctuation of its parts; provided they fall into the same connection, and serve the same uses their predecessors had done before.

According to the form and texture of these compositions, we conceive physical Beings denominated: so we are orthodox in this article of physiological faith. But we are reproved

for

for mifapplying the term *Man* to a part of him; becaufe we obferve, that no man can doubt of his own exiftence, and a little after place that exiftence in the mind, which is an individual that can be divefted of its Being by no power lefs than that which gave it. What then? has not the Man fuch a Being if his mind has it? May not we fay a Man has a frefh colour, becaufe he has it only in his cheeks; but none in his arms or his back? So the difpute turns upon a point of language rather than of phyfiology. For furely nobody can underftand us to imagine that when *Rice* was hanged, he was not divefted of his Manhood, or did not ceafe to be a Man. The fole queftion is, Whether the term *Man* may, upon any occafion, be applied to either of his parts after their feparation. Suppofe his body had been hung upon a gibbet in the little green near *Stamford-hill*, if on going along the road in dufk of evening with a friend, as my eyes are not very good, I fhould afk, Pray what is that fticks up in the middle of the common? Is it a tree? And he fhould anfwer, No: it is a Man hanging in chains. Would he be guilty of falfe language in his anfwer? Or fuppofe I afk *Whitefield* what he thinks is become of him: and he tells me, " Such a wicked Man,
" not

" not having received absolution from me, to
" be sure is gone to the Devil." Must we call
this an impropriety of expression, meerly because we are pretty sure the Devil has not got
both parts of the palpable Individual yet?

With regard to Agency, we hold as appears
by Note (b) on page 31, that in every human action the mind acts upon some corporeal organ or instrument, and having many of
them under command, she can by employing
them respectively affect things external, as
when we take up a book; or the body, as
when we wipe our face; or herself, as when
we recollect some past occurrence. All which
actions are ordinarily ascribed to the Man: for
we say the Man thinks, the Man wipes his
face, or the Man takes up a book. But if the
term *Man* belongs only to the palpable compound, it must include the whole of it, and
cannot be applied to the mind even together
with some of the limbs and organs exclusive
of the rest: so that the Man neither walks,
nor writes, because in the former his hands
perhaps hang dangling by his side; in the latter, his legs, like a couple of lazy curs, sit
doing nothing under the table. If we are to
be held to this rigorous physiological dialect,
perhaps no Man ever did a single thing in all
his

his life; because it would be difficult to assign any action whereto some parts of his composition were not wholly useless and unconcurrent.

As to the adverb *alternately*, I don't recollect where we have employed it: but if we have, I see no great harm done. Possibly Mr. *Monthly* takes a pipe sometimes, while sitting, like Fate, over the new-born babes of literature, to spin their future fortunes in the temple of fame. He whiffs and thinks, and thinks and whiffs again. In this case, might not we say the Man acts alternately. Sometimes upon his mouth to draw smoke into it, and sometimes upon his *Pericranium* to raise ideas there, now and then a little smoky too? or should we say the mind acts upon the pectoral and guttural muscles, they act upon the fuming weed in the tube, the exudations of that stimulate the sensory nerves in his palate, these communicate their motion to the brain, which acts upon the mind again, by raising up judicious observations for her to contemplate? Would this learned stile tend more to the entertainment and edification of our readers?

If our language, in all these particulars, has been incorrect, it will be good-natured in him

to

to set us right. In the mean time, as a man that makes aukward bows must go on with his aukwardness until his dancing-master can teach him to perform more genteely; so we may hope for indulgence in our vulgarity of expression, until our Master shall instruct us to deliver ourselves with better grace and elegance.

We have spent many more words in our defence than were employed in the attack: but it is always the case, that less trouble is requisite to puzzle a cause than to clear it up, and a man may make more tangles in a fine skain of thread in a minute, than he can undo again in an hour. We did not undertake it for the sake of our own credit, which has been much more raised than depressed by the labours of our good cousin Mr. *Monthly Comment*, who has said so many handsome things of us, that it would be vanity to repeat them; and a few freedoms ought not to be taken amiss, as they show an impartiality, that adds weight to what has been said in our favour. It is common to see two council fight like dog and bear at the bar, without thinking the worse of one another all the while; their strenuousness encourages clients. So our making a little noise with one another may turn to mutual

tual account; it may ferve, like the market-bell, to awaken the curiofity of cuftomers, and quicken the fale of both our wares. This benefit, if it accrues, we fhall be heartily glad of, in gratitude for the high encomiums beftowed on us; yet we own it will be purely accidental: for what raifed our follicitude, was the doctrine advanced, of the mind and material elements fluctuating and changing into one another; which feemed a revival, tho' we are willing to believe it was not intended as fuch, of the old atheiftical notion, that a perceptive and active Being might be formed of inert and fenfelefs principles. This feemed a matter of importance to us, well deferving our ferious care and endeavours to prevent; and engaged us to a replication, which upon all other accounts we fhould have judged needlefs.

F I N I S.

www.ingramcontent.com/pod-product-compliance
Lightning Source LLC
Chambersburg PA
CBHW020246240426
43672CB00006B/649